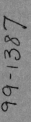

Circle Time Activities
For
Young Children

Deya Brashears
and
Sharron Werlin Krull

Dedicated To The Orinda Pre-School

Acknowledgments are made to:

Amy Flynn for her creative illustrations, Anita Obendorf for putting our musical notes on paper, Joan Brown and Norma Don for their time and assistance, Dick, Lea, Bill, J.P., Corrie.

Sales, Conference and Workshop Information contact:
Deya Brashears
Circle Time Publishing
P.O. Box 272652
Concord, CA 94520
Ph. 510-735-5173
Fax. 510-735-8768

Distributed by Gryphon House, Inc.
P.O. Box 217
Mt. Rainer, MD 20822

A WINNING COMBINATION

By
Deya Brashears

with
Lea
Brashears
and
Sharron
Werlin
Krull

DRIBBLE DRABBLE
A unique collection of age-appropriate, "geared for success" art experiences for ages 2 and up which focus on process rather than finished producuct

CIRCLE TIME ACTIVITIES
This innovative resource, color-coded by topic, provides finger plays, songs, games and activites for any gathering time, geared toward ages 2-8 years

MORE DRIBBLE DRABBLE
Back by popular demand, additional art experiences including illustra-tions!

ORDER TODAY!

Qty	Item	Price (CA tax)	Amount
	Dribble Drabble	$11.95 (.83)	
	More Dribble Drabble	$14.95 (1.09)	
	Circle Time Activities	$16.95 (1.23)	
	ADD SHIPPING: $3.95-1st book, 50¢ each add'l book		
	TOTAL ENCOLSED (Check or Money Order)		

Name _____

Address _____

City, State, Zip _____

MAIL TO:
Circle Time Publishing
P.O. Box 272652
Concord, CA 94520

About the Author

Circle Time Activities for Young Children (co-author Sharron Werlin Krull, 1981) is followed by Dribble Drabble...Art Experiences for Young Children (1985) and More Dribble Drabble (1992). Deya is a full time faculty member at Diablo Valley College in Pleasant Hill, CA. She was the Director/Teacher of the Orinda Pre-school for 14 years and an adjunct instructor at various Bay area colleges. Deya travels nationally to conduct workshops and seminars for parents and teachers. A graduate of Kent State University (B.S.) and University of Maryland (M.E.d.), Deya is currently working on her doctoral degree from University of San Francisco. She is listed in Who's Who among College and University professors and Who's Who in American Colleges and Universities and named to Cardinal Key Honorary Society. Deya was involved in the programs for Sesame Street and has designed, directed and taught special need programs. She wrote a parenting column for a local newspaper.

SHARRON WERLIN KRULL has a happy enthusiastic outlook which is contagious to those around her. Sharron's special appeal to children stem from her positive attitude towards life, her in-depth training, and her experiences in teaching. Since 1977 Sharron has been the Outdoor Teacher at The Orinda Pre-School. Sharron also teaches children's classes at several local Community Centers, Co-Directs a Summer Day Camp Program as well as organizing and Co-Directing a Kindergym program. Her experiences with Circle Time Activities for Young Children and her continual involvement with Early Childhood Education prompted a second publication, PLAY POWER...Games and Activities for Young Children (Co-Author Norma Don) in 1986. Since obtaining her B.S. degree in Elementary Education from Miami University of Ohio and teaching in the public schools, Sharron has augmented her education with graduate studies in Early Childhood Education and training in Sensory and Perceptual Motor Development. Sharron holds a Jr. College Teaching Credential and conducts teacher training seminars across the country. Her rich and active life include a love of sports, travel, sun and the ocean.

About the illustrator

AMY FLYNN is a talented illustrator, artist and graphic designer. She has illustrated both Circle Time Activities for Young Children and PLAY POWER...Games and Activities for Young Children. Amy's training is from California State University, San Jose, and from employment for two years with Hallmark. She is now with Current, Inc. in Colorado. Amy also does free lance work in stained glass. She and her Airedale Terrier live in Colorado Springs.

TABLE OF CONTENTS

INTRODUCTION

Circle Time is that special time when you gather around with several children to share songs, fingerplays, stories, games, rhythms and whatever that particular day brings. Besides offering a fun experience, Circle Time provides for a listening time, a time for auditory memory, a time to get to know each other, a time to sit quietly, a time for sensory experiences, and on and on. As you sit down with the children, they look at you with eager faces as if to say, "Well, what are we going to do today?" We, as preschool teachers have wished that we could turn to ONE book of ideas for Circle Time. We two preschool teachers have dreamed of such a complete, organized, and sequential book and our dream has become a reality in this book, **Circle Time Activities for Young Children.**

It is important to be flexible and spontaneous when conducting a Circle Time. Following the lead of the children usually stimulates a very successful activity; however, having something planned "just in case" gives you that added security that Circle Time will be fun and effective. The activities in this book have been tried, tested and proven as "attention-getters, "mind-expanders", and "eye-openers" for the young child. The activities have been divided into monthly chapters, beginning in September and ending in June, thus following the normal school calendar. All songs are indicated by Extra activities are listed at the end.

Have fun at Circle Time. We always do!

SEPTEMBER

yoga

Simple yoga exercises help the children settle down and focus on the new gathering time. If you begin each Circle with yoga, the children will expect it and learn to relax and enjoy this healthy activity. Yoga helps to develop awareness training, relaxation, strengthens the body, energizes the child, helps balance and muscle control. As you continue to use yoga, it will become second nature to the children and they will learn to come together for a more successful Circle Time.

lotus position

It is best to introduce yoga with the Lotus Position. The leader describes the position as she/he is actually demonstrating the exercise. For example:

Let's sit up straight with our legs crossed,
and our hands, palms up, on our knees or thighs.
Be sure to keep your back straight.

Close your eyes and mouth. Now, breathe in through your nose slowly. Keep your mouth closed.

Hold the air in and let it out through the nose slowly.

Let's try it again together as I count.

Breathe in - 1 - 2 - 3. Breathe out - 1 - 2 - 3.

To help the child get his back straight, say,
"Have you ever seen a puppet on a string? Imagine there is a string on the top of your head pulling you up so your spine is straight. Pull the imaginary string and sit up straight."

cleansing breath

Between yoga exercises, or at the end of an exercise, it is important to do a cleansing breath to energize the body before going on to the next activity. For example:

Close your eyes and mouth. Breathe in through your nose and hold.

Think about any unpleasant things that may have happened today - a fight with brother, a rushed morning, not being able to share a toy.

Now breathe out these unhappy feelings through your mouth. Now breathe in love and happiness and good feelings, and again breathe out any bad feelings.

1. The Cobra Snake

Lie face down on the floor with hands palms down by the shoulders, elbows on the ground.

Inhale, raising up the chest, straightening the arms and bending back, keeping the head up and shoulders down.

Exhale as you make the SSSSSS sound of the snake.

Keep stomach down and legs on the floor.

Come down slowly.

Relax.

2. The Lion

Kneel with hands on the knees, and spine straight.

Inhale deeply.

Force every bit of air from the lungs with a ferocious lion's roar. Look ferocious as you do it.

Repeat.

3. EEEEK and OOOOK

Kneel with hands on the knees and spine straight.

Form the word "eek" with your mouth, stretching your whole face into a big EEEEK. This stretches the whole face sideways.

Then form your mouth into the sound "oook", stretching the lips forward and drawing the whole face, eyebrows and neck forward into a mad OOOOK.

Repeat.

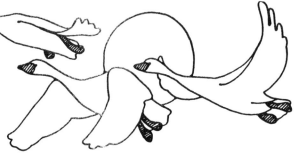

4. Bird

Birds love to fly high up in the sky. Balance on your tiptoes with your wings (arms) outstretched behind you, parallel to each other.

Bend slightly from the waist, and extend the head forward. Your hands are open and your fingers are spread apart.

Hold for a few minutes.

5. The Tree

Stand upright, feet together. Pretend that you are a marionette with a string holding your head and back straight.

Find a point on the wall directly in front of you. Concentrate on that point, and don't take your eyes off of it. It will help you to keep your balance.

As you concentrate, raise your right foot and place it on your left knee. Bend the right knee out to the right.

Raise your arms over your head. Straighten the arms, palms touching. Bring the arms in line with your ears.

Inhale through the nose, and exhale. Hold the position for a minute.

Inhale and come down on exhalation.

Repeat, using other leg.

6. The Balloon

It is helpful to introduce this position by using a balloon. Show the children what happens when you blow air into a balloon -- it puffs up. Then slowly let the air out and watch what happens -- it gets flat.

Ask the children to lie on their backs with eyes and mouths closed, and their arms and legs loosely outstretched.

Have them inhale deeply through the nose and let their tummy fill up like a balloon.

Place hands on your tummy and feel the air inside.

Now, breathe out slowly and let your tummy sink in like a balloon without air.

Repeat, and relax.

7. The Woodchopper

Stand with legs apart and hands clasped over your head.

Bend back, then forward and down, letting your arms fall between your legs as if holding a heavy axe.

Repeat.

As you raise your arms over your head, inhale through the nose. As you chop the wood, exhale through the mouth, pushing all the air out of the lungs.

8. Toy Soldier and Rag Doll

Stand up straight and tall, feet together, head erect, arms stiff at side, tummy in, and chest out.

Inhale through the nose and pretend you are a toy soldier guarding the castle gates.

Now exhale and relax your entire body. You are now a floppy rag doll. Bend at the waist, hang your head down, sway it from side to side, bend the knees and swing arms from side to side.

Inhale and repeat the soldier position.

9. Be A Camel

Get down on your hands and knees. Hunch your back up like a camel's hump. Pretend the center of your back is tied to a string that is hooked to the ceiling.

Keep your head down, and walk around on your hands and knees in a circle.

Now relax your back and curl up like a little ball by bringing your arms and knees in tight together.

Now be a camel again and see how high you can make your camel's hump.

10. Silver Bird

Have you ever seen a bird with its wings stretched way out to the side and soaring high up in the sky? Try pretending you are that silver bird.

Sit very straight on a low chair where your feet touch the floor.

Put your wings forward toward your face, and then way back out to the side again.

Flap your wings fast or slow. Close your eyes and pretend you are flying high in the sky.

11. Turtle

Do you know what happens to a turtle when it gets turned over on its back? It rolls harder and harder trying to flip itself over on its feet again.

Get down on a soft rug or mat and hug your feet tight to your body. Now roll back and forth. Now roll sideways. Straighten your legs and flip over on your tummy.

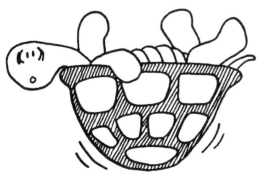

12. Arm-Breathing and Leg-Breathing

The children stand in a space of their choice. Breathe in deeply and exhale. Breathe in deeply again, letting the arms rise overhead. Exhale letting the arms return to the sides.

You may use this same exercise from a position where the children lie on the floor. Here, instead of letting the breath take the arms into space, let the breath take the legs into space.

13. The Frog

Sit on your heels in squatting position and balance on your tiptoes with hands wrapped over the head.

Try hopping around like a happy frog.

(Some children may not be able to balance on tiptoes. They should try doing this flat-footed.)

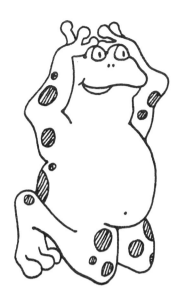

14. The Mountain

Sit in lotus position. Your legs will be the base of the mountain. Your arms and hands are the peak.

To make the mountain top, stretch your arms over your head, with fingertips touching and palms together.

Inhale and exhale slowly through your nose, and imagine that you are as still and quiet and peaceful as a mountain.

15. Recharging Yoga

Stand up, lie down, or sit in yoga position.

Tighten different parts of the body. Let them vibrate and then, very slowly, let them relax.

Start with the toes, then the legs, the tummy, arms and face. Then, finally, tense the entire body until it vibrates like a motor.

Slowly relax. We have recharged our entire bodies with new energy.

16. Sound Yoga

Sit in lotus position with eyes and mouth closed. Be very still and quiet.

Listen very carefully and chant the same sound as the leader. Listen carefully, because the leader might change the sound.

Inhale through your nose, and breathe out, saying the sound that the leader is saying. *(A-A-A-A-aah).*

Chant the sound until all the air is out of your lungs.

Inhale again, and recite another sound along with the leader. *(B-U-S-S; S-H-H-H-H; M-M-M-M, etc.)*

You can change the tone of the voice or the pitch to see if the children are listening carefully.

17. Take a Trip

The Circle Time leader will have to paint an imaginary picture for the children to visualize.

Have all the children sit in a relaxed lotus position, or lie down on their backs with eyes and mouths closed, and bodies totally relaxed.

One such imaginary picture might be a Magic Carpet Ride. Ask the children to imagine that they are sitting on a magic carpet and floating through the sky. The clouds are very white and puffy, and everything is very still. As the carpet goes through the clouds, everything seems foggy, or like being in the middle of cotton candy; but as you pass out of a cloud, everything is bright and blue, and very peaceful and clear. The clouds make the ride a little bumpy, and you feel yourself swaying on the carpet. Now you reach a very still and quiet place in the clouds.

Slowly open your eyes. You can now talk about your trip.

Ask what color (Suzie's) carpet was, or if it was hot or cold in the sky.

Another example of a trip might be rising slowly up and down on a wave in the sea. Imagine that everyone else is here on a wave in the sea too. Do you see all your friends drifting along beside you? Look, we are going up on a wave, and now down, up and then down. The sun is hot, and the water feels cool on our bodies. Here we go again -- up and down.

Slowly open your eyes. Again, discuss the colors seen or what was felt (sun on our shoulders, etc.)

All yoga exercises should end with a cleansing breath. Breathe in through the nose. Hold, and slowly let it out through the mouth.

getting to know each other

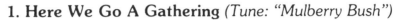

Becoming acquainted with each other, especially at the begining of the school year is important for each child and adult. Here are some "ice-breakers" that have worked well for us.

1. Here We Go A Gathering (Tune: "Mulberry Bush")

All: Here we go a gathering, a gathering, a gathering.
             Here we go a gathering to see who we can see.
Teacher: I see (Peter).
Child: I'm here.

Continue around the Circle until you have mentioned each child and he has responded with "I'm here".

Variation: Try saying names of fictitious characters — such as, (Superman). The children will answer, "He's not here." This enhances listening skills.

2. Where Is (Amy)? (Tune: "Are You Sleeping?")

Teacher: Where is (Amy)? Where is (Amy)?
Child: Here I am. Here I am.
Teacher: How are you today, (Amy)? (Shaking child's hand)
Child: Very well, I thank you.
Teacher: Run away; run and play.

Child runs back to Circle, and it's another child's turn.

3. Hickety-Pickety Bumble Bee (Chant)

All: Hickety-Pickety Bumble-Bee.
             Who can say his name for me?
Child: (Cathy)
Teacher: Let's all say it.
All: Cathy
Teacher: Let's clap and say it.
All: Ca-thy (clap-clap with syllables)
Teacher: Let's whisper it.
All: Cathy (softly)
Teacher: Let's turn off our voices and clap it.
All: (clap-clap)

Repeat chorus and go on to the next child.

4. Hello, Hello *(chant)*

> Hello, hello, hello and how are you?
> I'm fine, I'm fine and I hope that you are too.

Variation: Teacher sings the first line while the children answer back the second line. One half of the Circle sings the first line while the second half of the Circle answers back the second line.

5. There Was A Child Had A Name *(Tune: "B-I-N-G-O")*

> There was a child had a name and *(Sandy)* was her name oh.
> S-A-N-D-Y, S-A-N-D-Y, S-A-N-D-Y *(spell and clap)*
> And *(Sandy)* was her name, oh.

If name is shorter or longer than five letters, just fit it in.

6. Good Morning *(chant)*

> Good morning, good morning and how do you do?
> Good morning, good morning,
> I'm fine, how are you?

7. The More We Get Together
(Tune: "Have You Ever Seen A Lassie?")

> The more we get together, together, together,
> The more we get together, the happier we'll be.
> For your friends are my friends. *(point to others)*
> And my friends are your friends. *(point to self)*
> The more we get together, the happier we'll be.

Repeat

8. Good Day Everybody *(chant)*

Good day everybody, good day everybody
Good day, good day, good day.
Let's smile everybody, let's smile everybody,
Let's chase those frowns away.

9. Good Morning *(chant)*

Good morning, good morning.
How are you today?
Good morning, good morning.
It's time to sing and play.

10. Here We Are Together
(Tune: "Have You Ever Seen A Lassie?")

Here we are together, together, together, oh
Here we are together all sitting on the floor.
Here's *(Susan),* and *(Becky),* and *(Steven),* and *(John),* etc.

11. Sing Your Name *(Chant)*

Sing me, sing me, sing me your name.
Child sings: *(Cor-rie).*

12. Are You Here? *(Tune: "Twinkle, Twinkle Little Star")*

(Kevin, Kevin) are you here?
Child: Yes, yes I am here.

Continue around Circle.

13. Yoo-Hoo *(chanting tune)*

Yoo-Hoo *(Lea)*

Child fills in singing his own name.
Advanced Variation: Child echoes another child's name.

14. Guess Who

Sit in the Circle and the teacher identifies a child by what she is wearing, color of eyes, etc. and see if the children can guess who the teacher is thinking of.

15. Picture Clue

Hold up a picture of a child and see if the other children can identify the child by name.

16. Touching

Introduce yourself to each child personally and extend your hand. Then have each child tell you his name.
(Hi, I'm Patty. What's you name? Cathy)

17. Name Game

Have children form a Circle and sit down. Go around the Circle with each child saying his name, one after the other, in something other than a normal voice. Names may be shouted, whispered, sung, etc. This can also be done by clapping the rhythm of each child's name.
(Su-san clap, clap)

18. Oops

Hold up five fingers.
Start with pinky finger and oops is in curve between pointer and thumb. Each finger tip gets name on it.
(Lisa, Lisa, Lisa, Lisa, OOPS, Lisa)
Go back, *(OOPS, Lisa, Lisa, Lisa, Lisa)*

Continue around Circle.

OCTOBER
colors and shapes

Many children are just beginning to recognize their colors and shapes and we have found that early in the year works best for us to establish these distinctions. Below are some successful activities.

1.
Color Song

Guitar chords:
Children and Teacher:

Those children wearing blue *(or any other color being sung about)* sing:

D	**G**
Blue, blue, blue, blue,	
A	**D**
Who is wearing blue, today?	
G	**A**
Blue, blue, blue, blue,	
A1	**D**
Who is wearing blue?	

I am wearing blue, today

Look at me and you will say

Blue, blue, blue, blue

I am wearing blue.

Variation: Sing about body parts.
(Ex.: "Who is wearing brown hair?")

2. Draw a Circle *(Chant)*

Draw a circle. Draw a circle *(draw circles in the air with fingers)*
Round as can be
Draw a circle, draw a circle
Just for me.

Draw a square. Draw a square *(draw squares in the air)*
Shaped like a box
Draw a square, draw a square
With corners four.

Draw a triangle. Draw a triangle *(draw triangles in the air)*
With corners three.
Draw a triangle. Draw a triangle
Just for me.

3. Color Activities

A. Start with identifying the primary colors. See if the children can identify them.

    a. Go on color walks. Have the children pick out various colors or assign a few children to find things that are blue, a certain group to find things that are red. Come back to the Circle and share what they have found. Be sure the children put back the objects that they found.

    b. Play "I spy" with colors. *(Ex.: "I see someone with red tennis shoes and white socks on, who can tell me who.")*

B. Continue to secondary colors.

    a. Show what happens when you combine yellow and blue playdough or food coloring or tempera.

    b. Color games are good. *(Ex.: Candyland, Go Fish, Color Lotto)*

4. Griddily, Griddily

Teacher: "Griddily, Griddily I see something that you don't see and the color is *(red)*."

Children guess what you have in mind. The one who guesses gets to think of the next color-object.

5. Popsicle Sticks

Put various shapes on popsicle sticks. Hold up one at a time and ask the children to tell you the shape, color and flavor it might be if it were a popsicle.

6. Feely Box

"Feely Box" with face drawn on front. Cut mouth hole large enough for a hand to fit inside. Put in a shape *(start with circle, square, and triangle)*. Let child feel that shape and see if he/she can tell what shape it is. Later other shapes or objects can be used *(ex: a clothespin, sponge, feather, etc.)*

Another type of feely box is a box filled with tiny styrofoam bits and the shape can be buried within the styrofoam. A sock also makes a good feely box.

7. Blindfold Game

Blindfold one child and then give him/her a shape to feel and tell what it is. Take turns doing this. Later this can be used for textures and weight.

8. Symbol Reading

Have the children sit in a circle on the floor. Tell them they are going to read something and do the action.

Show a circle -- this might mean "to walk." A triangle might mean to skip, etc.

Hold up various shapes and have the children recall the action associated with the shape.

9. Draw Shapes

Draw shapes in the air and see if the children can guess what shape you are drawing. Let the children draw with you or have a turn trying to trick the other children.

10. Poster

Use any poster and ask the children to point to the various shapes within the poster. *(Ex.: a circle could be a wheel on a car)*

Go on a shape walk and identify various shapes as you go. Pick up shapes to share when you return to the Circle.

11. Body Shapes

Have the children spread out and make various shapes out of their bodies. *(Ex.:Make a circle, a triangle, etc. Let them be creative.)*

12. Walking Sticks

Try this story first with flannel-board figures.
Then give children toothpicks and paper shapes so they can "act out" the story as you read it aloud.

Six little sticks went out to play. The hot round sun shone down on them as they walked along in a very straight line, looking for some sand to play in.
(Sticks walk in a line on green grass. Sun shines.)
"Look at the round sun," said the sticks.
(Sticks "point" to the sun.)
"Lets' play here, and make shapes in the sand."
(Sticks arrive at brownish sandy area)
Four sticks lay down on the ground and make a square.
(Sticks join to create a square or are placed around the edge of a colored paper shape.)
Three sticks lay down and make a triangle.
(Sticks join to make a triangle)

(Similar narrative may be repeated for other shapes.)

"Look at the sky," said the sticks. "There are dark clouds. It's going to rain."
(Dark clouds appear above sticks.)
The sticks began to run as the raindrops came down with a splash on the sand.
(Rain comes down as sticks run away.)
The sticks slipped into an oval mud puddle. They got stuck and could not move.
(Sticks become "stuck" in an oval mud puddle.)
They had to wait until the rain stopped and the hot sun dried the mud.
(Rain stops, sky becomes blue, and sun appears.)
Then the sticks pulled themselves out and happily marched away in a straight line.
(Sticks march away in a line.)

13. Make a Ball

A little ball, a larger ball.
(Make three sequential sizes with fingers O O O).
A great big ball I see.
Now let us count the balls we've made.
One, two, three.

14. Sorting

Allow the children to sort objects according to size, shape or color. This might include buttons, bottle caps, keys, blocks, shells, rocks, beads, money, etc.

halloween

Halloween is a favorite holiday for many of us and there are numerous activities to choose from. Here are some to try.

1. Halloween Surprise *(Tune: "Sing A Song Of Sixpence")*

First you take a pumpkin *(arms for large pumpkin before tummy)*
Big and round and fat
Then you cut the top off *(pretend to slice)*
That will make the hat *(hand on head)*
Then you hollow out the
Nose and mouth and eyes. *(point to nose, mouth and eyes)*
Show it to the children for a *(resume first position)*
Halloween surprise!

2. Three Little Witches *(Tune: "Ten Little Indians")*

One little, two little, three little witches
Flying over haystacks, flying over ditches
Sliding down moonbeams without any hitches
All on Halloween night.

3. Halloween's Coming (Tune: "London Bridge")

Halloween will soon be here,
    Soon be here,
    Soon be here,
Halloween will soon be here,
Look out, children.

Witches riding on a broom,
    On a broom,
    On a broom,
Witches riding on a broom,
Look out, children.

Black cats howling on a fence,
    On a fence,
    On a fence,
Black cats howling on a fence,
Look out, children.

Goblins hiding in the dark,
    In the dark,
    In the dark,
Goblins hiding in the dark,
Look out children.

Skeletons clanking in a line,
    In a line,
    In a line,
Skeletons clanking in a line,
Look out children.

Trick-or-treaters everywhere,
    Everywhere,
    Everywhere,
Trick-or-treaters everywhere,
Look out children.

Strange things happening all around,
    All around,
    All around,
Strange things happening all around,
Look out children.

4. I'm A Mean Old Witch

5. Pumpkin Bells (Tune: "Jingle Bells")

Dashing through the streets
In our costumes bright and gay
To each house we go
Laughing all the way.
Halloween is here
Making spirits bright
What fun it is to trick-or-treat
And sing pumpkin carols tonight.

Oh, pumpkin bells, pumpkin bells
Ringing loud and clear
Oh what fun Great Pumpkin brings
When Halloween is here!

6. Three Little Witches (Chant)

Three little witches on Halloween night.
Danced and sang by pumpkin light.

First little witch sang a sweet little song
DUM-DITTY, DUM-DITTY, DING, DING, DONG!

Second little witch did a dance with her broom
One-two-three. Boom, boom, boom.

Third little witch did a trick with her hat
Tip it, tap it. Out flew a bat.

Three little witches on Halloween night.
Swish with their brooms -- out went the light.

7. Halloween Nite

8. Pumpkin Time

October time is pumpkin time *(Clasp hands before tummy like pumpkin)*
The nicest time of year
When all the pumpkins light their eyes *(Point to eyes)*
And grin from ear to ear.
Because they know at Halloween
They'll have lots of fun.
Peeking through windowpanes *(Peek through)*
And watching people run. *(Make fingers run)*

9. Jack-O-Lantern

I am a pumpkin big and round,
Once upon a time I grew on the ground.
Now I have a mouth, two eyes, and a nose.
What are they for, do you suppose?
When I have a candle inside burning bright,
I'll be a Jack-O-Lantern on Halloween night.

10. Three Little Pumpkins Sitting on a Fence

Three little pumpkins sitting on a fence
A witch came flying by
Ho-Ho-Ho or Hee-Hee-Hee, I'll take you all
And make a pumpkin pie.
*(Join hands and make a circle
on last line for the pie)*

-16-

11. Five Little Pumpkins

Five little pumpkins sitting on a gate
The first one said, "My it's getting late."
The second one said, "There's witches in the air."
The third one said, "I don't care."
The fourth one said, "Come on, let's run."
The fifth one said, "It's only Halloween fun."
So they sat up straight and lit their light,
And became Jack-O-Lanterns on Halloween night.

12. Boo

Boo! Boo! Boo! Boo!
I'm a ghost to scare you.
From Halloween town
I've come this night
All dressed from tip to toe in white
BOOoo! BOOoo! BOOoo!

13. Halloween Tree

I saw a Halloween tree
And someone was looking at me.
Black cats and bats
And witches too,
The ghosts and skeletons
All said, "Boo, woo -- ooo,
Woo-ooo, woo-ooo, Boo!"

14. One October Night

A witch, she went a-shopping   (turn around, walk in place)
One October day,
One October day.   (go through motions of
She bought some stew,   buying something)
And a new broom too.
One fine, clear October day.

A witch, she went a-sweeping   (sweeping motion)
One cleaning day,
One cleaning day.
She dusted her house   (dusting motion)
And chased out a mouse   (shooing away motion)
One busy cleaning day.

A witch, she set to stirring   (stirring motion)
At suppertime,
At suppertime.
She sat down to sup   (all sit down)
And ate it all up,   (pretend to eat)
At witch's suppertime.

A witch, she went to dressing   (dressing motions)
One midnight hour,
One midnight hour.
She straightened her hat,   (straighten hat)
Then patted her cat,   (bend down, patting motion)
One late midnight hour.

A witch, she went a-riding
One Halloween night,   (hands together, held out,
One Halloween night.   jog in place)
She took up her broom   (picking up motion)
And "ALA-KA-ZOOM!"
One moonlight Halloween night.   (all speak loudly, hands
                                                      (zoom up towards sky)

15. Witch Hunt

Teacher: I'm going on a witch hunt. Do you want to go?
　　　　　All right, let's go!

(slap thighs as in a tramping motion)

Teacher and children:

Oh look!
There's a brook.
Can't go around it.
Can't go over it.
Gotta go through it.
All right.
Let's go. *(swimming motion)*

Oh look!
There's a bridge.
Can't go round it.
Can't go through it.
Gotta go over it.
All right.
Let's go. *(pound chest)*

Oh look!
There's a tree.
Can't go round it.
Can't go through it.
Gotta go up it.
All right.
Let's go. *(climb thumb and index finger)*

Oh look!
There's a swamp.
Can't go around it.
Can't go over it.
Gotta go through it.
All right.
Let's go.
(inflate cheeks, punch in with index fingers)

Oh look!
There's a cave.
Let's go see what's inside.
All right.
Let's go *(climb down)*
Let's go softly *(tramping motion)*

Oh look!
I see two big eyes.
I see a big tall hat.
I feel something like a broom.
It looks like a witch.
It sits like a witch.
It is a WITCH!

(reverse all motions very fast as if being chased by the witch. Slam the door)

Whew!

16. The Goblin

A goblin lives in our house, in our house, in our house,
A goblin lives in our house all the year round.
He bumps
And he jumps
And he thumps
And he stumps
He knocks
And he rocks
And he rattles at the locks.
A goblin lives in our house, in our house, in our house.
A goblin lives in our house, all the year round.

17. Spooky Sounds

(Make a tape of these sounds and ask the children to identify)

1. wind, thunder and rain
2. cats yowling and fighting
3. pack of dogs, baying
4. door slam and something being dragged
5. creaking door or shutter
6. something ripping
7. fuse *(or fire)* burning and explosion
8. sawing
9. drops of water, dropping or plopping
10. object falling into water
11. space ships

18. Mr. Jack-O-Lantern

Mr. Jack-O-Lantern is very round and fat.
He has a yellow candle, lit right beneath his hat,
It makes his face look happy, and very, very bright,
When he winks and smiles at me
On spooky Halloween night.

19. Trick or Treat Game

Children take turns removing a slip of paper from a container. *(Decorated as a jack-o-lantern)*. If the slip of paper shows a picture of a Halloween treat *(candy, black cat cupcakes, candy corn, apple, raisins, nuts, etc.)*, the child remains sitting down. If the slip is marked "trick," the child must perform a stunt or do some sort of pantomime. *(Ex.: cry like a baby, twirl like a ballerina, wind up like a pitcher and throw an imaginary ball, sing a song, etc.)*

20. Halloween Finger Play

One little candle, burning very bright,
Lights my pumpkin on Halloween night.
Two little goblins, dressed in white,
Hide in the dark on Halloween night.
Three black cats scared with fright,
Yowl and howl on Halloween night.

Four black witches in moonlight bright,
Ride their broomsticks Halloween night.

Five little children run with all their might,
Tricking and treating Halloween night.

See the ghosts, goblins, and witches in flight.
Let's pretend they're real on Halloween night!

21. Five Little Jack-O-Lanterns

Five little Jack-O-Lanterns (one hand up)
Sitting on a gate
The first one said, (point to thumb)
"My, it's getting late."
The second one said, (pointer finger)
"I hear a noise."
The third one said, (middle finger)
"It's just a lot of boys"
The fourth one said, (ring finger)
"Come on, let's run."
The fifth one said (little finger)
"It's just Halloween fun."
"Puff" went the wind
And out went the light (close fingers into fist)
And away went the Jack-O-lantern
(open hand, fingers run behind back)
Halloween night.

22. Fat Old Witch

The strangest sight I've ever seen
Was a fat old witch on her flying machine.
The witch flew high.
The witch flew low.
The witch flew fast.
The witch flew slow.

She circled all around the town.
Then, turning left and turning right,
She disappeared into the night.
The strangest sight I've ever seen
Was a fat old witch on her flying machine.
Of course it happened on Halloween!

23. A Halloween Counting Poem

One scary witch is coming down the street.
She's tapping at doors and calling,
"Trick or Treat!"

Two black cats
Appear at the gate,
With arched-up backs,
They watch and wait.

Three jack-o-lanterns sit grinning in a row,
Their candles flicker
An eerie glow.

Four bats awake and begin to fly,
Swishing and swooping
Across the sky.

Five tree stumps in the shadows deep
Crouch like monsters
Ready to leap.

Six orange leaves float down through the air,
They rustle and whisper,
"Beware, beware!"

Seven gray clouds hide the moon from sight,
They stop, they hover,
They darken the night.

Eight white objects twist and twine.
Are they ghosts or sheets
On a line?

Nine little field mice scatter and run.
Spooky nights
Are not much fun.

Ten owls smile -- they know, you see.
It's Halloween and the
witch is ME!!

24. The Witch Rides

The witch is on her broomstick.
Riding very fast.
O-O-O Halloween at last.
The skeleton is dancing.
On his bony toes.
Tipping, tapping.
On and on he goes.
See the ghosts come floating.
White against the sky.
O-O-O They go drifting by.
See the funny goblins.
Dancing down the street.
Knocking, knocking,
Crying "Trick or treat."

25. Halloween Poem

I know I saw a spooky witch
Out riding on her broom.

I know I saw a goblin thing
Who's laughing in my room.

I think, perhaps, I saw a ghost
Who had a pumpkin face.
And creepy cats
And sleepy bats
Are hiding everyplace.

It doesn't matter where I look
There's something to be seen.

I know, it's October
So I think it's Halloween!

26. Witch Witch

Witch, witch where do you fly?
Over the moon and under the sky.
Witch, witch what do you eat?
Little black apples from Hurricane Street.
Witch, witch what do you drink?
Vinegar, blacking and good red ink.
Witch, witch, where do you sleep?
Up in the clouds where pillows are cheap.

27. Black Cat

The black cat yawns
Opens her jaws
Stretches her legs
And shows her claws.

Then she gets up
And stands on four
Long stiff legs
And yawns some more.

Lifting herself
On her delicate toes
She arches her back
As high as it goes.

She lets herself down
With particular care
And pads away
With her tail in the air.

28. In A Pumpkin Patch

Three little pumpkins
Lying very still,
In a pumpkin patch
On a great big hill.

This one said, "Oh, I'm
very, very green;
But I'll be orange
For Halloween."

This one said, "Oh, me!
Oh my! Today I'll be
A pumpkin pie."

This one said, "Oh,
I'm on my way
To be a
Jack-O-lantern gay."

29. Carve a pumpkin for the children to see. Let them feel the pumpkin and the seeds inside. Prepare a pumpkin delight and roast the seeds.

NOVEMBER

health and nutrition

It is important to instill in the children a sense of respect for our bodies. We have listed some experiences that are fun and yet convey the message that our bodies are important and need to be taken care of.

1. **So Early In The Morning** *(Tune: "Mulberry Bush")*

This is the way we brush our teeth, brush our teeth, brush our teeth,
This is the way we brush our teeth,
So early in the morning.

Continue using other activities, such as: comb our hair, wash our face, etc.

2. **Dirty Hands** *(chant)*

Dirty hands are such a fright
See, I washed mine clean and bright! *(hold hands out, palms up)*
Mother says it is quite right
To wash them morning, noon and night.

3. **Bath Time** *(chant)*

After a bath, I try, try, try
To wipe myself dry, dry, dry. *(rub upper arms with hands)*
Hands to wipe and fingers and toes, *(hold hands out,
   palms up, then point to toes)*
Two wet legs and a shiny nose, *(hands on thighs, then point to nose)*
Just think how much less time I'd take
If I were a dog and could shake, shake, shake. *(shake body)*

4. **Brushing Teeth** *(chant)*

Up and down and round and round *(move right pointer up and down,
   and round before mouth)*
I brush my teeth to keep them sound.
To keep them sound and clean and white *(point to teeth)*
I brush them morning, noon and night.

5. **Going to Bed** *(chant)*

This little boy (girl) is going to bed. *(lay pointer in palm)*
Down on the pillow he lays his head *(thumb acts as pillow)*
Covers himself with the blankets so tight *(wrap fingers around "boy")*
And this is the way he sleeps all night. *(close eyes)*
Morning comes, and he opens his eyes *(open eyes)*
Throws back the covers, up he flies *(open fingers)*
Soon he is up and dressed and away *(pointer stands straight)*
Ready for school and ready for play.

6. **Classifying Foods**

   Cut out pictures of various foods and mount them on tagboard. Make a pile for each food group *(breads, protein, etc.)* Hold up each card and see if the child can put it into the proper food group.

7. Talk about good nutrition. Explain that candy, cookies, etc. are really not good for the body and the teeth. Talk about what foods **are** good for the body and the teeth.

8. Ask a dentist to visit the school to discuss the proper ways of brushing teeth and to suggest to children various snacks that would be good for them to eat.

9. Get a giant-sized toothbrush and tooth model, or make one out of cardboard. Talk about different kinds of teeth and tell the children the names of the various kinds of teeth. Explain what each type of tooth does for us. *(Ex.: cutting, grinding, etc.)*

   With the large models, show the children the proper way to brush teeth, that is in a circular motion.

10. **Identification Food Group Game**

    1. Make a large four-color "rug" on which the children can classify foods.

    2. Have the children identify the color and the food group; red for the meat group, green for the vegetable group and the fruit group, yellow for the milk group and orange for the bread and cereal group.

    3. Collect empty food containers and ask the children questions about them. *(Do you think this is a bread, or a vegetable? etc.)*

    4. The child can then place it on the proper section of rug according to the color.

11. **Guess the Food**

    1. Put several fruits and vegetables into a bag that is open just enough to allow the child's hand to enter.

    2. The child chooses a food, feels it and must identify it by texture alone. If he's right, he gets another turn. If he's wrong, he loses a turn.

12. **Tasting**

    1. Gather small pieces of food that the children will be familiar with. Show them the selection so that they won't be afraid it will be "yucchy."

    2. Have a child close his eyes and give him a small piece of one of the foods and see if he can identify it.

13. Growing

1. Explain to the children where our fruits and vegetables come from.

2. Show pictures of planting the seeds, taking care of the plants, and harvesting them.

3. Let each child sample a piece of whatever fruit or vegetable you talked about.

Each child should have the actual experience of planting a seed and seeing it grow.

Doctor Visit

14. Have a doctor visit the school and explain what is done on a well-visit checkup. He can show his stethescope, otoscope, etc.; and possibly allow the children to use them with his supervision. Children can role play doctor throughout the year.

15. Act out the various hygiene activities and see if the children can guess what you are doing. Then see if they can dramatize one and if you can guess what they are doing.

16. Explain how important it is to get enough rest and how our bodies require so much sleep in order to stay healthy.

body parts

Learning the various body parts can be a lot of fun as we have discovered in the experiences listed below.

1. Sing A Song (Tune: "Mulberry Bush")

Now I know the parts of me,
Parts of me, parts of me.
Now I know the parts of me,
Listen, look and see.

(touch appropriate parts and sing)

This is what I call my head,
Call my head, call my head.
This is what I call my head,
Listen, look and see.

Continue adding various body parts.

2. Eyes, Nose, Ears, Mouth

Chant in singsong fashion with no fixed tune.

Eyes, nose, ears, and mouth,
Eyes, nose, ears, and mouth,
Eyes, nose, ears, and mouth,
See the parts of me.

Make up additional verses using different body parts.

SONG:

PUT YOUR FINGER IN THE AIR

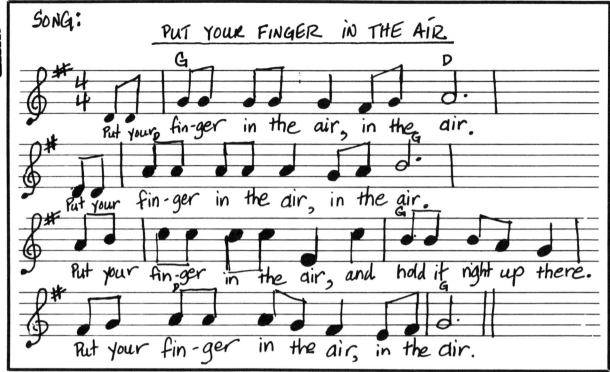

Put your fin-ger in the air, in the air.
Put your fin-ger in the air, in the air.
Put your fin-ger in the air, and hold it right up there.
Put your fin-ger in the air, in the air.

EXTRA VERSES:

Put your finger . . .

2. on your **nose,** and feel it as it grows
3. on your **chin,** that's where the food slips in
4. on your **ear,** and leave it there a year
5. on your **toe,** and leave it a day or so
6. on your **finger,** that's where we'll let it linger

4. **Where Is Thumbkin?** *(Tune: "Are You Sleeping?")*

Where is Thumb-kin? Where is Thumb-kin? *(place hands behind back)*
Here I am, here I am. *(show one thumb, then other)*
How are you today sir? *(bend one thumb)*
Ver-y well I thank you. *(bend other thumb)*
Run and play, run and play. *(wiggle thumbs away)*

Where is . . . . . Pointer *(second finger)*
Where is . . . . . Tall Man *(middle finger)*
Where is . . . . . Ring Man *(fourth finger)*
Where is . . . . . Pinky *(fifth finger)*
Where is . . . . . The Whole Family *(whole hand)*

5.

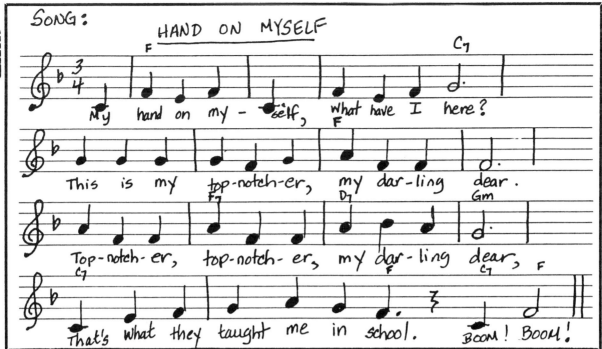

SONG: HAND ON MYSELF

My hand on my-self, what have I here?

This is my top-notch-er, my dar-ling dear.

Top-notch-er, top-notch-er, my dar-ling dear,

That's what they taught me in school. BOOM! BOOM!

EXTRA VERSES:

2. eye winker	(hand on eye)
3. sweat browser	(hand on brow)
4. horn blower	(hand on nose)
5. soup strainer	(hand on mustache)
6. bone crusher	(hand on mouth)
7. chin chopper	(hand on chin)
8. rubber necker	(hand on neck)
9. chest sweller	(hand on chest)
10. bread basket	(hand on stomach)

On "boom, boom," slap each hand on thigh.

6.

SONG: CLAP YOUR HANDS

Clap, clap, clap your hands, clap your hands to-geth-er.

clap, clap clap your hands, clap your hands to-geth-er.

EXTRA VERSES:
1. Touch, touch, touch your toes . . .
2. Drum, drum, drum your feet . . .
3. Flap, flap, flap your arms . . .
4. Tap, tap, tap your knees . . .
5. Stand up very tall and touch the sky together . . .

7. Action Chant

Stoop and stand,
Hands in the air.
Wave your arms,
Now touch your hair.
Bend your trunk
And touch the floor--
Hold it while
I count to four:
1 - 2 - 3 - 4
Slowly stand
And reach far out.
Grab a friend.
Now swing about
1 - 2 - 3 - 4

8. I'm Glad I'm Me *(chant)*

I'm glad I'm me. I'm special, look and see.
My feet can run and dance and walk.
My ears can hear, my mouth can talk.
My hands and arms can stretch out wide.
My face shows how I feel inside.

Refrain: Healthy, that's me, and I'm going to be
always taking care of me, so I can
grow up happily.

I'm glad I'm me. I have a family
We help each other when we're sad
We might get mad, we're often glad
We make up a country strong and free
Americans, all we're proud to be.

9. Teacher asks children to touch various body parts. Ex.: "Touch your eyes, nose, ears," etc. Move down the entire body and get more complex as the children learn about their bodies.

Variation: Play Simon Says using body parts. Ex.: "Simon says pat your head, shake your left leg, wriggle your right hand," etc.

10. Making Sounds

Ask the children to make various sounds using different body parts. Ex: hands can clap, slap, snap, etc. Feet can stomp, slide, shuffle, etc.

11. Dancing

Have the children sit in a circle. Let various parts of the body dance. *(Ex.: put on slow music and let the children dance with their fingers, their hands, toes, arms, legs, head, whole body.)*

12. Playing the Mirror Game

1. Have the children look at their bodies in the mirror. Allow ample time to let the children move their muscles and bodies so that they can see how they work.

2. Have two children stand face to face. One of them is to be the mirror. Give the other child something to do. *(Ex.: wash your face, wash behind your ear, brush your teeth.)* Then the child who is the mirror mimicks the actions of the other child, using the opposite side of his body as he faces the child looking into the mirror.

13. Muscles

Let the child feel an arm or leg muscle in action. Talk about movement.
Open mouth, close eyes, move fingers and thumbs, etc.

14. Bones

Ask the children what bones they can feel on themselves *(finger, ankle, legs, etc.)*

Find the backbone on another child. Explain that bones hold us together.

Show a skeleton or pictures of one.

15. Heart and Blood

Let child listen to his heart by placing his head and ear on another child's chest.

Let the children find blood vessels on their bodies and explain how the blood travels throughout the body and goes into the heart and lungs.

16. Fingernail Care

Discussion can center around use of the fingernails and how they need to be cared for. Include the following points:

1. Fingernails protect the sensitive ends of the fingers.

2. They help us pick up small items.

3. Dirt and germs may collect under them.

4. Dirt and germs on fingernails can be taken into the mouth by children who are still sucking their fingers or eating food held in their hands.

5. Dirt and germs from fingernails can be passed on to others in hand-to-hand activities.

17. Moving the Body

1. Ask the children to move various body parts. Begin with the easy and obvious ones *(arms, legs, eyes, mouth, etc.)* Move onto more complicated parts such as chest, ankles, elbows, etc.

2. Space awareness: ask the children to make their bodies curl up into a ball. Now use up more space by stretching out your arms and legs. Continue to suggest various positions, such as, "put your arms between your knees, place one foot on the other knee," etc.

18. I Have Two Eyes To See With

I have two eyes to see with, *(touch eyes)*
I have two feet to run with, *(run in place)*
I have two hands to wave with, *(wave)*
And nose I have but one, *(touch nose)*
I have two ears to hear with, *(touch ears)*
And a tongue to say good day, *(stick tongue out)*
And two red cheeks for you to kiss, *(touch cheeks)*
And now I'll run away.

19. Hinges

I'm made of hinges 'cause everything bends *(bend body parts at joints)*
From the top neck *(touch neck)*
Way down to my ends *(touch feet with hands)*
I'm hinges in front and I'm hinges in back,
But I have to be hinges or else I would crack.

This rhyme should be preceded with an explanation of what a hinge is and an example of one.

20. Finger Movements

Demonstrate the following finger activities before the children try them:

1. Make a fist and open one finger at a time.
2. Extend fingers and make a fist, closing one finger at a time.
3. Place the hand on a table or floor and raise one finger at a time.
4. Close fingers together and spread them apart as far as possible.
5. Touch the tip of the thumb to each finger.
6. Number or letter each finger joint and touch each number or letter with the thumb.

21. Touch Your Nose

Touch your nose, touch your chin
That's the way this game begins.
Touch your eyes, touch your knees
Now pretend you're going to sneeze.
Touch your hair, touch your ear
Touch your two red lips right here.
Touch your elbows where they bend
That's the way this touch game ends.

22. Knock, Knock

Ring the bell *(pull child's hair)*
Knock at the door *(knock on child's forehead)*
Peep in the windows *(open eyes wider)*
Lift the latch *(push up tip of nose)*
Open the door *(open up child's mouth)*
And go down in the cellar and eat apples
   (fingers skip down throat to Adam's Apple)

Can follow with this addition:
   Chinchopper *(touch child's chin)*
   Nose dripper *(touch nose)*
   Eye Peeper *(touch eye)*
   I love you! *(give child a big hug)*

23. Touch Exercise

I'll touch my hair, my lips, my eyes
I'll sit up straight and then I'll rise;
I'll touch my ears, my nose, my chin
Then quietly sit down again.

24. Fun Body Part Chant

Toe-d, Toe-d, Tippy Toe
Hee-ly, Hee-ly, Hi-lee Bank
Shinny, Shinny, Shinny Shank
Knee, Knee, Knick-a-Knack
Thigh, Thigh, Thick-a-Thack
And a Belly, Belly, Belly-Whack!

25. Clap Your Hands

Clap, clap, clap your hands
   As slowly as you can.
Clap, clap, clap your hands
   As quickly as you can.

Shake hands . . . .
Roll hands . . . .
Rub hands . . . .
Wiggle your fingers . . . .
Pound your fists . . . .

26. Rickety, Tickety

Rickety, tickety, look at me.
How many fingers do you see?

Ex.: Hold up two fingers. If child answers "one" say,
"One you say, but there are two."

Repeat till correct, then praise child.

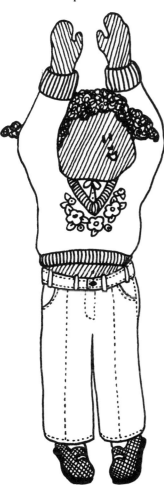

27. Right Hand, Left Hand

This is my right hand, I'll raise it up high. *(right hand over head)*
This is my left hand, I'll touch the sky. *(left hand up)*
Right hand, *(show right palm)*
Left hand, *(show left palm)*
Roll them around. *(roll hands over and over)*
Left hand, *(show palm)*
Right hand, *(show palm)*
Pound, pound, pound. *(pound fists together)*

28. Head and Shoulders

Head and shoul-ders, knees and toes, knees and toes.
Head and shoul-ders, knees and toes, knees and toes.
Eyes and ears and mouth and nose,
Head and shoul-ders, knees and toes, knees and toes.

Touch the body parts as you say the verse in different ways, as;
faster each time
leave out different body parts

29. Body Play Verses

1. Look!
   This is me.
   I stand right here
   For all to see.
   My arms stretch out,
   My legs kick high.
   I even bend back
   To see the sky.

2. Legs are the most marvelous limbs,
   Attached to both hers and hims.
   They're made for bending,
   Lifting,
   Jumping.
   They even do a little thumping.

3. Fingers, fingers, everywhere.
   Fingers blinking in the air.
   Fingers making little holes.
   Fingers tying little bows.
   Fingers learning to button and snap.
   Fingers on hands that like to clap.

4. Forward roll my shoulders--
   I'm curled up like a ball
   Backward go my shoulders--
   Now I'm standing tall.

30. Ten Little Fingers

I have ten little fingers and they all belong to me. *(hands upright)*
I can make them do things, would you like to see?
I can shut them up tight. *(shut them up into fists)*
Or open them wide. *(open them wide)*
I can put them together, or make them all hide. *(close fists together)*
I can make them jump high. *(swing hands above head)*
I can make them go low. *(swing hands down low)*
I can fold them up quietly and hold them just so. *(place in lap)*

31. Two Little Feet

Two little feet go tap, tap, tap.
Two little hands go clap, clap, clap.
One little leap up from the chair,
Two little arms go up in the air.
Two little hands go thump, thump, thump.
Two little feet go jump, jump, jump.
One little body goes round and round.
One little child sits quietly down.

32. I Wiggle

I wiggle my fingers, *(Wiggle fingers)*
I wiggle my toes, *(Wiggle toes)*
I wiggle my shoulders, *(Wiggle shoulders)*
I wiggle my nose. *(Wiggle nose)*
Now no more wiggles are left in me.
So I will be still as still can be.

33. Wink--Wink

Make one eye go wink, wink, wink. *(Wink one eye)*
Make two eyes go blink, blink, blink. *(Blink both eyes)*
Make two fingers stand just so; *(Hold up two fingers)*
Then ten fingers in a row. *(Hold up ten fingers)*
Front and back your head will rock! *(Rock head back and forth)*
Then your fists will knock, knock, knock. *(Thump fists together)*
Stretch and make a yawn so wide; *(Children stretch and yawn)*
Drop your arms down to your sides. *(Let arms fall)*
Close your eyes and help me say *(Close eyes)*
Our very quiet sound today.
Sh . . . . Sh . . . . shhhhhhhhhhhhhhhhhhhhhhhhh!

34. Stretch, Stretch

Stretch, stretch, way up high. *(Reach arms upward)*
On your tiptoes, reach the sky. *(Stand on tiptoes and reach)*
See the bluebirds flying high. *(Wave hands)*
Now bend down and touch your toes. *(Bend to touch toes)*
Now sway as the North Wind blows. *(Move body back and forth)*
Waddle as the gander goes! *(Walk in waddling motion back to seats)*

35. Open, Shut Them

Open, shut them; open, shut them.
Give them a clap.
Open, shut them; open, shut them.
Lay them in your lap.
Creep them, creep them slowly upward
To your rosy cheeks.
Open wide your shiny eyes
And through your finger peek.
Open, shut them; open, shut them;
To your shoulders fly.
Let them, like the little birdies,
Flutter to the sky.
Falling, falling, slowly falling,
Nearly to the ground,
Quickly raising all your fingers,
Twirling them around.
Open, shut them; open, shut them,
Give them a clap.
Open, shut them; open, shut them.
Lay them in your lap.

36. Stretch Up High

Stretch up high,
Stretch down low,
Raise your arms,
And away we go.

Make a circle in the air,
Sweep your arm around,
Now the other -- do the same
And jump up off the ground.

We like to bend.
We like to stretch.
We make our muscles strong.
Bend, stretch
Bend, stretch
All the whole day long.

First I bend my knees
Then I stand up tall.
Down, up, down, up
Like a rubber ball.
First I'm short
Then I'm tall.

37. Ready to Listen

Let your hands go clap, clap, clap. *(Clap hands three times)*
Let your fingers snap, snap, snap. *(Snap fingers three times)*
Let your lips go very round. *(Make lips round)*
But do not make a sound.
Fold your hands and close each eye. *(Follow action indicated)*
Take a breath . . . . and softly sigh: *(Follow action indicated)*
Ah ----------------------

38. Stand Up Tall

Stand up tall, *(Children stand)*
Hands in the air. *(Raise hands)*
Clap your hands, *(Clap three times as words are said)*
Make a frown. *(Children knit brows)*
Smile and smile, *(Children smile)*
And flop like a clown! *(Children relax with arms dangling)*

39. Puppet Imitation

Leader sits with a large puppet that has a representative human body. She makes the puppet do various movements *(touch nose, stomp foot, wave, etc.)* and asks the children if they can imitate what the puppet is doing with their own bodies.

Children can also be the demonstrator with the puppet.

40. Body Language

(Act out)

Hips wiggle
Tummies sag
Shoulders shrug
   Tongues wag
   Toes tap
   Feet patter
   Scalps tingle
     Teeth chatter
     Chests heave
     Backs ache
       Hair curls
       Nails break
       Arms fold
       Legs jump

Ankles sprain
Hearts pump
Noses twitch
   Hands clap
   Elbows bend
   Finges snap
   Skin wrinkles
     Knuckles crack
     Knees knock
     Lips smack
       Thumbs twiddle
       Eyes blink
       Heads nod
       Brains think!

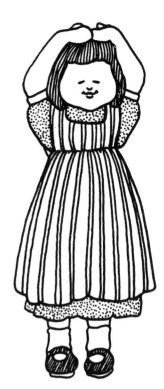

41. My Hands

My hands upon my head I place
Upon my shoulder, upon my face.
At my waist and by my side
And then behind me they will hide.
Then I raise them way up high
And let my fingers swiftly fly.
Then clap, one-two-three
And see how quiet they can be?

42. Reach For The Sky

Clap your hands, touch your toes,
Turn a-round and put your fin-ger on your nose.
Flap your arms, jump up high,
Wig-gle your fin-gers and reach for the sky.

43. Little Thumbs Go Marching

Little thumbs go marching,
little thumbs go marching
Little thumbs go marching,
don't you think that's fine?

(Add other body parts)

44. Flying Fingers

Flying fingers, flying high
Flying way up to the sky.
Flying fingers, flying low
Find a place you like to go.

(Everyone lies on their backs)

Flying feet, flying high
Flying way up to the sky.
Flying feet, flying low
Find a place you like to go.

45. Oliver Twist

Oliver Twist, Twist, Twist,
Can't do this, this, this.
Touch your knees, knees, knees,
Touch your nose, nose, nose,
Touch your hair, hair, hair,
Touch your toes, toes, toes.

46. Fingerplay

Fee Fi Fo Fum: Here's my fingers, here's my thumb.
Fee Fi Fo Fum: Fingers gone, so is thumb.

Thanksgiving

All people young and old need to reflect on all the things that we are thankful for. Here are some songs and games to share.

1. Thanksgiving Day

Over the river and through the wood,
To grandfather's house we go.
The horse knows the way
To carry the sleigh
Through the white and drifted snow.

Over the river and through the wood,
Oh, how the wind does blow!
It stings the toes
And bites the nose,
As over the ground we go.

Over the river and through the wood,
Now grandmother's cap I spy!
Hurrah for the fun!
Is the pudding done?
Hurrah for the pumpkin pie!

2. To Grandma's House *(Tune: "The Farmer In The Dell")*

To Grandma's house we go,
 (Make two fists and move them up and down as riding)
Heigh ho, heigh ho, heigh ho,
We're on our way with horse and sleigh,
Through fluffy drifts of snow.

Oh, what a trip to take!
She'll have a chocolate cake,
There'll be some pies *(Hands clasped before stomach)*
Of monstrous size
And chestnuts we can bake.

To Grandma's house we go,
Heigh ho, heigh ho, heigh ho.
What lovely things Thanksgiving brings,
The nicest things we know.

3. Five Turkeys In A Tree

Five fat turkeys are we. *(One hand up)*
We slept all night in a tree. *(Hands clasped above head)*
When the cook came around,
We couldn't be found,
That's why we're here, you see. *(Right hand up)*

4. A Hunting We Will Go

A hunting we will go,
A hunting we will go,
Heigh-ho the dairy-o,
A hunting we will go.

A hunting we will go,
A hunting we will go,
We'll catch a little fox,
And put him in a box,
And then we'll let him go!

Hunt for other animals and have them do silly, funny things. (*Ex.: fish-dish, bear-cut his hair, pig-jig, giraffe-laugh, dinosaur-squeeze him 'till he roars, dog-jog, etc.*)

5. Five Fat Turkeys

Five fat turkeys were sitting on a fence. (*One hand up*)
The first one said, "I'm so immense." (*Point to thumb*)
The second one said, "I can gobble at you." (*Pointer finger*)
The third one said, "I can gobble, too." (*Middle finger*)
The fourth one said, "I can spread my tail." (*Ring finger*)
The fifth one said, "Don't catch it on a nail." (*Little finger*)
A farmer came along and stopped to say (*Pointer finger of other hand*)
"Turkeys look best on Thanksgiving Day."

Variation of last two lines:
Out came the cook with a great big pan (*Arms in pan form*)
Away flew the turkeys, their tails in a fan. (Fingers fly away)

6. Gobble, Gobble

A turkey is a funny bird,
His head goes wobble, wobble.
And he knows just one word,
Gobble, gobble, gobble.

7. Table Stretches

Every day when we eat our dinner,
Our table is very small. (*Show size with hands*)
There's room for daddy, (*Hold up tall finger*)
And mother, (*Hold up pointer finger*)
And baby, that is all. (*Hold up little finger*)
But when Thanksgiving Day comes,
You can't believe your eyes.
For that table stretches (*Stretch arms*)
Until it is this size!

8. Two Little Turkeys

There were two little turkeys
Roosting in a tree, one cold November night.
Along came a fox, a hungry old fox,
And gave them a terrible fright.

Said the first little turkey,
"Gobble, gobble, gobble, we must think of a plan
To get rid of that fox, that hungry old fox,
Just as soon as we can."

Said the second little turkey,
"Gobble, gobble, gobble, I wish Farmer Brown would come
And shoot that fox, that hungry old fox,
With his big, black, shiny gun."

Soon out of the woods came Farmer Brown,
"Bang! Bang! Bang!" went his gun,
He shot that old fox, that hungry old fox,
And made him run, run, run.

Two little turkeys roosting in a tree,
One cold November night,
Dream of a fox, a hungry old fox,
Who gave them a terrible fright.

DECEMBER

christmas

This is the holiday season and we hope you will enjoy some of these new ideas and old favorites.

1. Christmas carols are always good to sing. Children especially love Rudolf and Jingle Bells.

2. Christmas is Coming

SONG: **CHRISTMAS IS COMING**

Chorus:

clap, clap your hands and sing out with glee, for Christ-mas is com-ing and hap-py are we.

Verse 1:

our stock-ings we'll hang while were a-sleep, Down thru the chim-ney will san-ta Claus creep.

Verse 2:   He'll empty his pack and up he will go,
Calling his reindeer will dash away home.

3. S-A-N-T-A *(Tune: "B-I-N-G-O")*

There is a jolly, jolly man
And Santa is his name-o.
There is a jolly, jolly man
And Santa is his name-o.
S-A-N-T-A *(clap, clap, clap, clap, clap) (clap five times in rhythm)*
S-A-N-T-A *(clap, clap, clap, clap, clap)*
S-A-N-T-A *(clap, clap, clap, clap, clap)*
And Santa is his name-o.

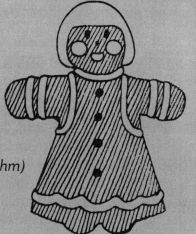

4. We Wish You A Merry Christmas

We wish you a Merry Christmas,
We wish you a Merry Christmas,
We wish you a Merry Christmas,
And a Happy New Year.

Let's all do a little clapping,
Let's all do a little clapping,
Let's all do a little clapping,
And spread Christmas cheer.

Verse (2) Jumping
Verse (3) Hopping
Verse (4) Stomping

Suggestion: On chorus, join hands and ring around circle. On verse, stand still and do motions. Repeat chorus after each verse. Add your own.

5. Santa Claus Is Coming To Town

You'd better watch out, you'd better not cry,
you'd better not pout, I'm telling you why.
Santa Claus is coming to town.
He's making a list and checking it twice.
Gonna find out who's naughty or nice
Santa Claus is coming to town.

He sees you when you're sleeping.
He knows when you're awake.
He knows if you've been bad or good
So be good for goodness sake.

Oh! You'd better watch out
You'd better not cry
Better not pout, I'm telling you why
Santa Claus is coming to town.

6. Frosty The Snowman

Frosty the Snowman was a jolly happy soul
With a corn cob pipe and a button nose and
Two eyes made out of coal.
Frosty the Snowman is a fairy tale, they say,
He was made of snow, but the children know how he came to life one day.

There must have been some magic in that old silk hat they found.
For when they placed it on his head, he began to dance around.

Oh, Frosty the Snowman was alive as he could be,
And the children say he could laugh and play just the same as you and me.

Thumpety, thump thump, thumpety thump, thump
Look at Frosty go.
Thumpety, thump thump, thumpety, thump, thump
Over the hills of snow.

7. Ten Little Angels *(Tune: "Ten Little Indians")*

1 little, 2 little, 3 little Angels
4 little, 5 little, 6 little Angels
7 little, 8 little, 9 little Angels
10 little Angels in the band.

Wasn't that a band on Christmas morning
Wasn't that a band on Christmas morning
Wasn't that a band on Christmas morning
Christmas morning coming soon.

8. Five Little Bells

Five little bells, hanging in a row.
The first one said, "Ring me slow."
The second one said, "Ring me fast."
The third one said, "Ring me last."
The fourth one said, "I'm like a chime."
The fifth one said, "Ring me at Christmas time."

9. Here's Santa

Here's Santa, jolly and gay. *(Hold up thumb on left hand)*
He'll soon be on his way.
Here's Mrs. Santa, making toys *(Hold up thumb on right hand)*
For all good girls and boys.
Come Dancer, Prancer, Dasher, and Vixen. *(Hold up four fingers
    on left hand and point to them)*
Come Comet, Cupid, Donner and Blitzen. *(Hold up four fingers
    on right hand and point to them.)*
Now, away to your housetop, *(Point to a friend)*
Clickety-clop, clickety-clop, clickety-clop. *(Clapping motion,
    loud, soft, softer)*

10. Santa

When Santa comes down the chimney *(Downward motion with hands)*
I should like to peek *(Peek through fingers)*
But he'll never come, no never *(Shake head)*
Until I'm fast asleep. *(Palms together beside head)*

11. Five Little Reindeer

Five little reindeer, prancing in the snow,
Waiting for Santa to say, "Let's go!"
The first little reindeer said, "Let's be on our way."
The second little reindeer said, "It will soon be Christmas day."
The third little reindeer said, "The sleigh is full of toys."
The fourth little reindeer said, "They're for all the girls and boys."
The fifth little reindeer said, "We'll travel far tonight."
Then out came Santa with his "Ho, Ho, Ho!"
And the sleigh and the reindeer were soon out of sight.

12. Christmas Toys

A ball, *(make a circle with hands)*, a book *(open it)*, a tooting horn
   (pretend to be tooting a horn).
I hope I'll get on Christmas morn.
A ball to bounce, *(bounce it)*
A book to read *(pretend)*
A horn to toot *(pretend to toot)*
When I see Santa I'm going to say,
Please bring me these toys on Christmas day.

13. Snow Men Fade Away

Six little snowmen standing in a row
Each with a hat and a big red bow.

Six little snowmen dressed for a show
Now they are ready, where will they go?

Wait till the sun shines, soon they will go
Down through the fields with the melting snow.

14. Christmas Tree

Here is Bobby's Christmas tree *(stand right hand upright)*
Standing right up tall.
Here's a pot to hold its trunk *(cup left hand under right hand)*
So that it won't fall.
Here are balls to make it gay *(thumb and pointer fingers in ball formation)*
One ball, two balls, see?
And here are two bright candles red *(right pointer and middle fingers upright)*
To trim the Christmas tree.

15. Five Little Reindeer

One, two, three, four, five little reindeer *(hold up fingers, one at a time)*
Stand beside the gate.
"Hurry Santa," said the five
"So we will not be late."
One, two, three, four, five little reindeer *(hold fingers again)*
Santa said, "Please wait.
Wait for three more reindeer *(hold up three more fingers)*
And then that will make eight."

16. This Little Present

This little present goes to Mary *(thumb)*
This little present goes to Ned *(pointer)*
This little present goes to Harry *(middle finger)*
And this little present goes to Ted. *(ring finger)*
This little present cried "Boo Hoo Hoo. *(little finger)*
Please put me into the Christmas stocking too!"

17. Clap Your Hands

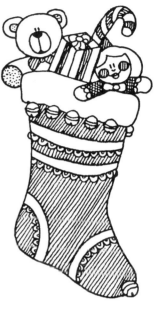

Oh clap, clap your hands, and sing out, with glee, *(clap)*
For Christmas is coming, and merry are we.
Now over the snow come Santa's reindeer
They scamper and scamper to bring Santa here.
We'll hang up our stockings and when we're asleep!
Down into our houses old Santa will creep.
He'll fill all our stockings with presents and then
Santa Claus and his reindeer will scamper again,
So clap, clap your hands and sing out with glee *(clap)*
For Christmas is coming and merry we are.

18. The Chimney

Here is the chimney, *(fist)*
Here is the top. *(other hand over fist)*
Open the lid, *(remove hand)*
Out Santa will pop! *(pop up thumb)*

hanukah

All of the songs below can be chanted to any tune.

1. Oh Dreidel

Oh Dreidel, Dreidel, Dreidel
We made it out of clay.
Oh Dreidel, Dreidel, Dreidel
With you we like to play.

2. Candles of Hanukah

Burn little candles
Burn, burn, burn
Hanukah is here.
Burn little candles
Burn, burn, burn
Burning bright and clear.

3. Light the Candles

Light the candles
Light the candles
Light the candles
At Hanukah time
   (pretend to light candles)

Spin the dreidel
Spin the dreidel
Spin the dreidel
At Hanukah time
   (pretend to spin the dreidel or get
   a real one and do it.)

Dance together
Dance together
Dance together
At Hanukah time
   (join hands and dance by
   moving around in a circle)

4. Happy Day

Happy Day, joyful day
Hanukah is here.
Happy Day, joyful day
Hanukah is here.

5. Dreidel Song

Twirl about, dance about
Spin, spin, spin
Turn dreidel turn
Time to begin

Soon it is Hanukah
Fast dreidel fast
For you will lie still
When Hanukah is past.

6. Hanukah

Who fought Antiochus?
Tell me please.
I know, I know
The MacCabees.

Who saved the Temple?
Tell me please.
I know, I know
The MacCabees.

Who gave us Hanukah?
Tell me please
I know, I know.
The MacCabees.

JANUARY
community helpers
& safety

What would we do without the garbage man or the fireman? Children can learn how so many people help us in our daily lives through some cute activities we have grown to enjoy. Here they are.

1. Smokey The Bear

Song:

SMOKEY THE BEAR

Smo-key the bear, smo-key the bear,

Prowl-in and a growl-in and a snif-in the air.

He can smell a fire, be-fore it starts to flame.

That's why they call him Smo-key, and that's how he got his name.

2.
Traffic Light

Red says STOP.
   (Hold up left hand in "stop" gesture)
Green says GO. *(Right arm motioning)*
Yellow says WAIT. *(Hold up index finger)*
You'd better go slow.
When I reach a crossing place
   (Cross arms at wrist)
To the left and right I turn my face.
I walk, not run across the street. *(Use fingers)*
And use my head to guide my feet.
   (Point to head and feet)

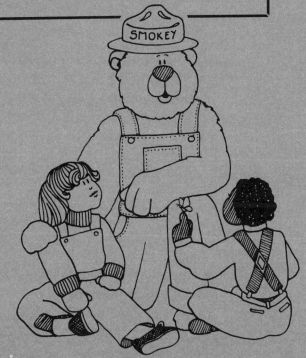

3. Ten Tall Firemen

This can be acted out during dramatic play
or used as a fingerplay.

Ten tall firemen sleeping in a row.
"Ding" goes the bell and down the pole they go.
They jump into their fire trucks with no delay.
The sirens warn everyone to get out of the way.

With water from big hoses they put the fire out.
"Hurrah, hurrah, brave firemen!" all the people shout.
Then back to the station go ten tired men
To sleep until the bell wakes them up again.

4. Red Light

Red light, red light
What do you say?
I say, "Stop" and stop right away.

Yellow light, yellow light
What do you mean?
I mean "Wait" until the light turns green.

Green light, green light
What do you say?
I say "Go" but first look both ways.

Thank you, thank you
Red, yellow, green.
Now I know what traffic lights mean.

5. Fire Drill

Teacher should discuss the "whys" of drills and the necessity for them.
Children should have several practice drills.

6. Traffic Signs

(1) Draw traffic signs onto cardboard or purchase various signs.
(2) Introduce the various signs to children so that they can be familiar with their meanings.
(3) Signs can be placed outside and children can obey their meaning while riding bikes, etc.

7. Our Friend

Tell the children that they are going to play a game about being lost. Talk about how it feels to be lost. Ask who might help them find their way home; ask how they could tell someone where they live; ask how they could let their parents know they are all right. They may need help by saying, "Do you think a policeman could help you?" "How would you tell him where you live?" They may want to dramatize this experience.

8. Mail

Five little letters lying on a tray. *(Extend fingers of right hand)*
Mommy came in and took the first away. *(Bend down thumb)*
Then Daddy said, "This big one is for me."
I counted them twice, now there were three.
Brother Bill asked, "Did I get any mail?"
He found one and cried, "A letter from Gale." *(Bend down middle finger)*
My sister Jane took the next to the last.
And ran upstairs to open it fast. *(Bend down ring finger)*
As I can't read, I'm not able to see
Whom the last one's for, but I hope it's for me!
    (Wiggle the little finger, then clap hands)

9. Traffic Policeman

The traffic policeman holds up his hand,
    (Hold up hand, palm forward)
He blows the whistle, *(Pretend to blow whistle)*
He gives the command. *(Hold up hand again)*
When the cars are stopped, *(Hold up hand again)*
He waves at me.
Then I may cross the street you see.
    (Wave hand as if indicating for someone to do)

10. I Am A Tailor

I am a tailor making clothes. *(Pretend you are sewing)*
Stitch, stitch, stitch.
My needle goes.

I am a policeman. I stand just so. *(Stand straight and tall)*
Telling cars to stop. *(Hold out your left arm to stop cars)*
Telling cars to go. *(Motion with your right arm for cars to move ahead)*

I am a cobbler mending a shoe. *(Pretend you are hammering)*
Rap, tap, tap.
And it's just like new.

11. Look Both Ways

Step on the corner.
Watch for the light.
Look to the left.
Look to the right.
If nothing is coming,
Then start and don't talk.
Go straight across.
Be careful and walk.

12. Walking Home

When I walk home from school today,
I'll walk the safe and careful way.
I'll look to the left.
I'll look to the right.
Then cross the street when no car is in sight.

13. Traffic Lights

Do you know what traffic lights say to you?
Do you know what traffic lights say to do?
Yellow says, "Be careful." *(Hold arm straight out)*
Green says, "You may go." *(Lower arm)*
But red is most important, *(Raise arm up)*
It says, "STOP" you know.

transportation

We all know about cars but what about airplanes, trains and even rocket ships? Look out below for some exciting adventures on all of these vehicles.

1. Down By The Station (Traditional Tune)

Down by the station, early in the morning,
See the little pufferbellies all in a row,
See the station master pull the little handle.
Chug, chug, toot, toot! Off we go.

2. The Train

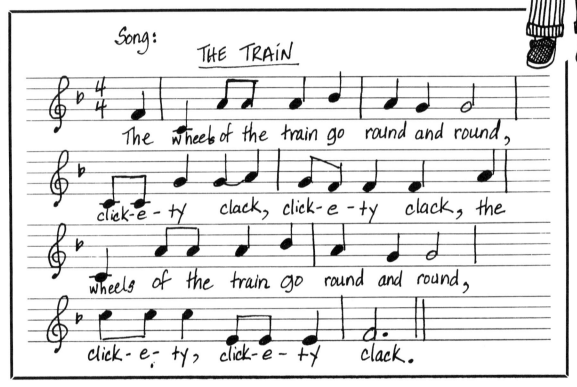

Song:

THE TRAIN

The wheels of the train go round and round,
click-e-ty clack, click-e-ty clack, the
wheels of the train go round and round,
click-e-ty, click-e-ty clack.

2. The engineer toots his horn,
    Toot . . . *(pull imaginary cord)*
3. The crossing gates come right down.
    Clang . . . *(arms up, elbows bent,*
        hands move down toward each other)
4. The people on the train get bumped around,
    Bump . . . *(body moves up and down)*

3. Row, Row, Row Your Boat (Traditional Tune)

Row, row, row your boat gently down the stream.
Merrily, merrily, merrily, merrily, life is but a dream.

Song:

ROCKET SHIP

Put on your space hel-met, Put on your space suit.

strap an ox-y-gen tank to your back.

We'll take a long trip in our rock-et ship.

Thou-sands of miles to the moon and back.

Thou-sands of miles to the moon.

5. I've Been Working On The Railroad (Traditional Tune)

I've been working on the railroad.
All the live long day.
I've been working on the railroad.
Just to pass the time away.
Can't you hear the whistle blowing?
Rise up so early in the morn.
Can't you hear the captain shouting
Dinah blow your horn.
Dinah won't you blow, Dinah won't you blow,
    Dinah won't you blow your hor-or-orn.
Dinah won't you blow, Dinah won't you blow,
    Dinah won't you blow your horn.
Someone's in the kitchen with Dinah. Someone's in the kitchen
    I know-oh-oh-oh.
Someone's in the kitchen with Dinah.
Strumming on the old banjo.
And singing Fe-Fi-Fiddly-i-oh.
    Fe-Fi-Fiddly-i-o-o-o.
        Fe-Fi-Fiddly-i-oh.
Strumming on the old banjo.

6. The Diesel Train *(Traditional Scale Song)*

The diesel train is coming, yes, now she's in plain sight.
Her bell rings out a warning. Her light is burning bright.
She's flying down the main line. At last she must slow down.
She rolls into the station. Her brakes make screeching sounds.
Ding, ding, ding, ding, ding, ding, ding, ding. "All a-board."

7. The Wheels On The Bus *(Traditional Tune)*

The wheels on the bus go 'round and 'round,
  (Rotate hands around each other)
Round and 'round, 'round and 'round
The wheels on the bus go 'round and 'round,
All over town.

2. Doors -- open and shut
3. Windows -- up and down
4. Money -- clink, clink, clink
5. Driver says -- move on back
6. Baby -- says boo, hoo, hoo
7. Mommy says -- shh-shh-shh
8. Daddy goes rock, rock, rock
9. Wipers -- swish, swish, swish.

8. Train

Here is the train *(Make a fist out of hand for train)*
And here is the track *(Hold left arm level)*
Choo-choo forward!
Choo-choo back! *(Place fist on arm and move forward and back)*
Here are the wheels
Going clackety-clack. *(Rotate hands around each other)*
POOF! goes the smoke
From the big smokestack! *(Move hands up quickly in mushroom shape)*

9. Airplane

The airplane has great big wings. *(Arms outstretched)*
Its propeller spins around and sings. *(Make one arm go)*
"VVVVV"
The airplane goes up; *(Lift arms)*
The airplane goes down; *(Lower arms)*
The airplane flies high *(Arms outstretched, turn body around)*
Over our town.

10. Engine On The Track

Here is the engine on the track. *(Hold up thumb)*
Here is the coal car, just in back. *(Hold up pointer)*
Here is the box car to carry freight. *(Hold up middle finger)*
Here is the mail car. Don't be late! *(Hold up ring finger)*
Way back here at the end of the train *(Hold up little finger)*
Rides the caboose through the sun and the rain.

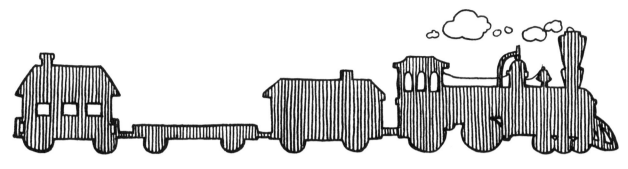

11. Engine, Engine

Engine, engine number nine, going down Chicago line,
If the train goes off the track, will I get my money back?

12. Let's Play Automobile

Teacher reads the verses while the children act them out.

Time to take a little ride.
Open the door and get inside.
  (Everyone pretends to open door and sit down)
Now the engine starts to hum.
Shakes a bit, goes brr . . . brr . . . brrrum!
  (Everyone on hands and knees, hums and shakes)

Then the tires go around
Rolling faster on the ground.
  (Everyone make circles in the air with arms)
Turn the steering wheel just so
To take us where we want to go. *(Everyone turns a steering wheel)*
OOOH! It's raining, splattering down!
Hear the windshield wiper's sound.
  (Everyone nods head from side to side clucking tongues in rhythm)

Turn the lights on, see them blink!
Did you know headlights could wink? *(Everyone winks)*
My! This road is full of bumps.
Ups and downs, and, oops, more jumps. *(Everyone jumps up and down)*
Our gas tank's low, our tires need air.
Look! A station over there! *(Everyone points)*
Listen to the air pump ring --
PSHT, PSHT, air goes in, then ping! *(Everyone imitates sounds)*
From pump to hose to empty tank,
What a lot of gas we drank! *(Everyone gurgles)*
Time to turn around and then,
Soon we'll all be home again.
  (Everyone turns around, then steps out of car)

13. Little Red Caboose

Little red caboose, chug, chug, chug.
Little red caboose, chug, chug, chug.
Little red caboose behind the train, train, train.
Smoke stack on his back, back, back, back.
Coming down the track, track, track, track.
Little red caboose behind the train. WOO! WOO!

14. Bridges

The bridges go up and the boats go under.
  (Knees are up and hands are boats that go under)
The bridges go down and SWOOSH go the cars.
  (Knees go down and cars go over knees)

FEBRUARY
valentine's day

A favorite time to tell someone he is special. Here are some of our favorites.

1. Love Is Something *(chant)*

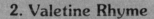

Love is something if you give it away,
Give it away, give it away.
Love is something if you give it away,
You end up having more!
It's just like a magic penny.
Hold it tight and you won't have any.
Lend it, spend it, and you'll have so many,
They'll roll all over the floor.
For love is something if you give it away,
Give it away, give it away.
Love is something if you give it away,
You end up having more!

2. Valetine Rhyme

Look who's coming down the walk.
Mr. Postman, won't you stop?
Knock, knock, knockety-knock.
Anyone at home?
A Valentine for you has come.
One for Jack, one for Mom.
One for Dad and one for Tom.
Knock, knock, knockety-knock.
Anyone at home?
A Valentine for you has come!

3. Pretty Valentine

To every little friend of mine.
I'll send a pretty Valentine.
   (Make heart shape with thumbs and pointers)
You'll find a message, if you'll look. *(Open palms)*
I'll use an envelope for this. *(Two fists together)*
I'll write my name, then seal a kiss.
   (One hand closes on fingers of other hand)

What color shall I give to you?
Orange, purple, green or blue?
Yellow or pink? White or red?
Or maybe a lacy one instead.

4. How Many Valentines?

Valentines, Valentines;
How many do you see?
Valentines, Valentines;
Count them with me:
    One for Father. *(Hold up thumb)*
    One for Mother. *(Pointer finger)*
    One for Grandma, too. *(Hold up middle finger)*
    One for Sister. *(Ring finger)*
    One for Brother. *(Little finger)*
And here is one for you!
    (Make a heart shape with thumbs and pointer fingers)

5. Roses Are Red

And don't forget these favorite famous two lines . . .

Roses are red, violets are blue,
Sugar is sweet and so are you.

feelings and emotions

Feeling angry or sad are feelings that everyone has whether they are young or old. All feelings are okay to have and it is important for children to learn to be aware of their feelings and to eventually identify them. Help the children to understand that *everyone* feels afraid, angry, lonely, etc. Try some of the activities below to get children to open up about their feelings.

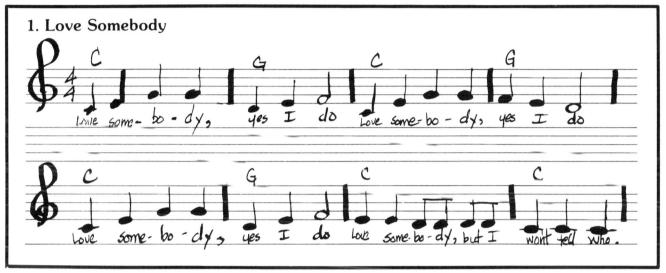

1. Love Somebody

Love some-bo - dy, yes I do Love some-bo - dy, yes I do

Love some-bo - dy, yes I do Love some-bo - dy, but I wont tell who.

Procedure:

1. It is nice to have children sit in a circle for this song, perhaps linking arms.
2. First hum the melody or chant and then sing it out loud as written.
3. After the first verse, substitute for the word "love" the word "hug". Encourage the children to respond to each other affectionatley and physically.
4. Discuss how you feel when you like or love someone. Discuss people you like, and what you do when you like somebody. Try to get them to think of other affection words for the song *(touch somebody, kiss, etc.)* but accept most any ideas they come up with and sing the song using these suggestions.

Variation:

1. A nice follow-up would be to quietly hold hands around the circle and send a "message" *(hand squeeze)* all the way around the circle.

2. The Laughing Song (chant)

A joke, a joke, oh what a joke I heard the other day.
I told it to a friend of mine to hear what he would say.
Well, you know I thought his sides would split! He went into a laughing fit.
A laugh, a laugh, oh what a laugh! Ha Ha, it went this way:
Ha ha ha ha ha ha ha ha ha ha ha ha ha ha ha ha ha ha ha ha ha etc.

Repeat song and change second line. These are some possibilities:

I told it to a little girl	Tee hee hee hee hee hee hee hee hee
I told it to my Grandpa-pa	Heh heh heh heh heh heh heh heh heh
I told it to a jolly fat man	Ho ho ho ho ho ho ho ho ho
I told it to a hoot owl	Hoo hoo hoo hoo hoo hoo hoo hoo hoo
I told it to a little dog	Bow wow wow wow wow wow wow wow wow

3. Guess How I Feel

Concept: Our bodies express our feelings.

Procedure: Call out an emotion and a body part that can be used to express it. Let the children individually or in small groups express the emotion with the body part named. Sounds such as growls, screams, laughs may help express the emotion; but only the body part indicated may be used.

Examples: Show joy with hands and arms only. Show fear by facial expression. Be surprised by using your head position only. Include other emotions such as love, anger, hate, loneliness, using other parts of the body.

After children have had an opportunity to express emotions this way, help them focus on specific feelings and actions: Have you ever seen someone do this? Have you done it? Let's watch for this and you tell me when you see someone showing how he feels with his body.

Variations: Let one child express an emotion, and let the rest of the class guess what it is. Children may work as partners. One child expresses an emotion and the other describes what the first child is feeling.

4. The Talking Body

Concept: We can use our bodies to send messages to others.

Procedure: Ask the children to show you how they would use their hand to say "stop"; how they would use their head to say "yes" or "no"; how to use their shoulder to say "I bumped the door"; eyes to say "I don't understand"; eyes or shoulder to say "I'm waiting" or "I'm angry"; ear to say "I hear something"; waist to say "I'm dancing"; finger to say "come here"; nose to say "I smell something"; legs to say "I'm slipping."

Then ask: How do parts of your body indicate or show how you feel or think? How does your nose show that you have a cold? How does your finger show it has been cut?

5. Face Language

Select pictures from a magazine which might express various feelings, such as loneliness, anger, fear, sadness, etc. Hold them up individually and see if the children can identify them. Ask each child to put on a feeling face and see if the other children can guess what she is feeling. Mirrors help children to see themselves with feeling faces.

6. Dream Music

Ask children to close their eyes and play soft gentle music such as Chopin, or Debussy and ask the children to describe how that music makes them feel. Then use other types of dramatic music such as scores from operas, operettas, or disco and then ask how this type of music makes them feel.

7. Sharing Feelings

Spontaneous and beautiful discussion can occur if you share one specific feeling at a time with the children. For example: "One time when I was a little girl, I felt very angry with my baby brother because he was getting all the attention and I wasn't."

Then the children will usually open up and talk about one time when they felt angry, or hurt inside, or lonely or happy or sad. It is important to define the particular feeling specifically and then not to deviate from it onto other feelings. Children can learn at an early age to define their feelings, and that feelings are neither right or wrong, and that we all have all those feelings at one time or another. Sometimes children will feel relieved to know that even his teacher has felt scared of the dark.

Tom

8. Angry (act out)

Angry, angry, angry!
So angry that I kick the air.
Then stamp my feet and pull my hair.
Now isn't it curious?
After feeling so furious . . .
I feel very good once more!

senses

Sensory experiences are an essential part of any program that deals with young children. These experiences are super, try them.

1. Sight

a. Find The Missing One

Show several objects such as different animals, different colored blocks, various shapes, etc. Talk about each one separately and then cover them with a cloth. Say "Abra-Kadabra" and wave hand over cloth. Remove one object from under the cloth and do not let the children see what you have removed. Then see who can guess which one is missing.

This can be made more complicated by using unrelated objects or removing more than one object.

b. Learning Relational Concepts

Have a box for the children to see. Talk about the various parts of the box. The top, bottom, side, inside, etc. Then get a doll and allow the children to touch the doll. Place the doll on top of the box and ask the children to describe where the doll is. Then put it inside, under, below, behind. Discuss each relationship with the children. Then let the children change positions and act as teacher.

2. Hearing

a. Ding-A-Ling

Everyone sits in a circle holding imaginary telephones to their ears. Using the children's names and their phone number's the teacher calls out a name and number and say's, "Ding-A-Ling." The "phoned" child answers and the teacher and child carry on a conversation. It's then another child's turn to be phoned.

b. Listening Walk

Children and teacher take a walk for the sole purpose of listening for various sounds. Some sounds that they might hear are birds, the sound of the wind, rustling leaves, lawn mowers, animals, machinery, etc.

c. **One Knock, Yes. Two Knocks, No.**

The child who is "It" is blindfolded. The rest of the children think of an object. The blindfolded child asks questions pertaining to the object such as, "Is it black or soft?" The other children answer with one knock for "yes" and two knocks for "no" until the child can guess what the object is. The child does not have to be blindfolded if the children can keep the object in mind. This activity is best for older children.

d. **Our Own Voices**

Make tape recordings of the children's voices both when they are aware of it and when they are not. Play back the tape and see if they can identify their own voices.

e. Play songs on an instrument or on a tape and see if the children can identify the song.

f. Have the children close their eyes and listen to the sounds around them. For example: clock ticking, voices, birds, etc.

g. **Mystery Noise**

Collect a group of noise makers, such as bell, rattles, whistles, sandpaper, horns, a timer, etc. Have the children close their eyes and see if they can identify the sound without looking. If the temptation is too great, and they **must** peek, make the noise behind a barrier.

h. **Common Sounds**

Tape some common household activities such as bacon sizzling, clanging dishes, beating eggs, washing dishes, a clothes dryer, a car motor, brushing teeth, flushing the toilet, the telephone, and taking a shower, and see if the children can identify the sounds.

i. **Recognizing High And Low Sounds**

Play a middle C and then ask the children to listen carefully to the same note. Now play another note that is higher and tell them that it is a higher note. Now play a lower note and tell them that this is a lower note. Now play a higher and/or lower note and see if they can tell which it is. Let them experiment.

j. Have the children make sounds and see if others can guess. For example: motor, sneeze.

3. Smell

a. Identify Smells

Use baby food jars and punch holes in the lid and add various smells to the jars. For example: cloves, mints, petals, sawdust, onions, apples, etc. See if the children can identify these smells.

A variation of this activity is to make duplicates of these smells and see if the children can match the smells.

b. Take a "smell walk" and discover the various smells in our environment, such as leaves, flowers, dirt, grass, fruit, water, etc.

4. Touch

a. How Do Things Feel?

Use objects differing in texture and hardness such as feathers, foam rubber, cork, metal, satin, burlap, sandpaper, marshmallows, etc. Let each child see these objects. Then have one child close his eyes and give the child an object from the group above. He should describe the object and then guess what it is. Let everyone have a turn and then let them test each other. If they peek, put the object into an old bag or sock so that they cannot see it.

b. Give the child two contrasting textures to feel and let him talk about the differences. For example: one is smooth, one is rough, one is large, one is small, soft, hard, fuzzy, bumpy, flat, etc.

c. See if children can identify each other with blindfolds on. Blindfold one child and ask another to sit in front of the blindfolded one. Let the blindfolded child touch only the face and see if she can identify the child.

5. Taste

Have a variety of foods such as apples, popcorn, cereal, peanut butter, etc. Have the child close his eyes and put a small piece of food in the mouth and see if he can identify what it is. Have the child hold his nose as he eats and then see if he can identify it.

6. Our Five Senses

Our ears tell us when folks are cheering.
We call this sense our sense of *(hearing)*.
To use this sense both day and night,
We need our eyes for the sense of *(sight)*.
We use our hands to feel and clutch.
And we call this the sense of *(touch)*.
To use this sense as you can tell,
I need my nose. This is the sense of *(smell)*.
When eating food in no great haste,
We use this sense and call it the sense of *(taste)*.
We have named each sense,
There are mainly five.
Hearing, smell, sight, taste and touch,
Tell us that we are alive.

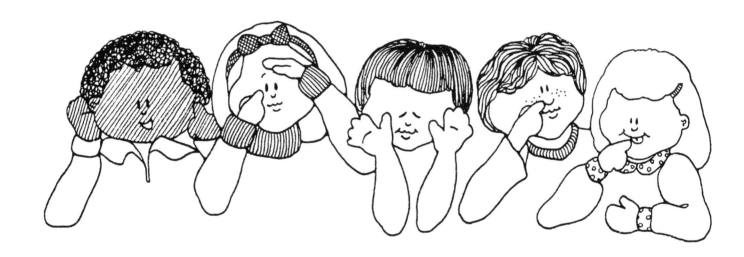

MARCH
animals

Animals are an integral part of every curriculum and below are a few of our favorite selections. These are divided into animal groups for your convenience.

1. Wide-Eyed Owl

The wide-eyed owl *(Circle eyes with fingers)*
Has a long pointed nose, *(Extend forefinger in front of nose)*
And two pointed ears, *(Hold up fingers on either side of head)*
And claws for his toes. *(Crook fingers)*
When that owl looks at you, *(Circle eyes again)*
He flaps his wings *(Flap arms up and down)*
And says, Whoo, Whoooooooooo!!

2. Baby Bird

Here's a ba-by bird-ie, he's hatching from his shell.

Out comes his head, and then comes his tail.

Now his legs he stretch-es, his wings he gives a flap.

Then he flies and flies and flies, now what do you think of that?

Down, down, down, down, down, down, down, down BOOM!

--65

3. I Love My Rooster

I love my little rooster, my rooster loves me.
I love my little rooster by the cottonwood tree.
I love my little rooster, he says cock-a-doodle-doo.
Dee-doodle-dee-doodle-dee-doodle-dee-doo.

Add verses using children's suggestions for animals and letting
them make the sounds of that animal.

4. Five Little Ducks *(Traditional Tune)*

Five little ducks went out to play.
Over the pond and far away.
Mother duck called with a quack, quack, quack.
Four little ducks came back, came back.

Four little ducks.......
Three little ducks.......
Two little ducks.......
One little duck.......
No little ducks went out to play.

5. Two Little Blackbirds

Two little blackbirds
Sitting on a hill. *(Point fingers up)*
One named Jack, *(One hand forward)*
And one named Jill. *(Other hand)*
Fly away, Jack. *(One hand behind back)*
Fly away Jill. *(Other hand)*
Come back, Jack. *(Return one hand)*
Come back, Jill. *(Return other hand)*

6. Little Duck

I am a little duck that goes quack, quack, quack.
  (Make hand be duck's mouth and it quacks)
And I've got lots of feathers on my back, back, back.
  (Wave hands near bottom to indicate tail feathers)
And when I go down to the lake, I wiggle and I wobble and I shake,
  shake, shake.*(Wobble and shake around like a duck)*
And when I go to sleep at night, *(Pretend to be sleeping with hands as pillows)*
I close my eyes very tight.
But in the morning when I wake,
I wiggle and I wobble and I shake, shake, shake.

7. Three Little Ducks That I Once Knew *(Traditional Tune)*

Three little ducks that I once knew.
A fat one, a skinny one, a yellow one too.
But the one little duck with a feather on his back
He ruled the others with his quack, quack, quack!

Down to the meadow they would go.
Wibble-wobble, wibble-wobble to and fro.
But the one little duck with the feathers on his back.
He ruled the others with his quack, quack, quack.
He ruled the others with his quack, quack, quack.

8. The Hen and The Chickens

Good mother hen sits here on her nest,
Keeps the eggs warm beneath her soft breast,
Waiting, waiting day after day.
Hark! There's a sound she knows well.
Some little chickens are breaking the shell.
Pecking, pecking, pecking away.
Now they're all out. Oh, what a crowd!
Good mother hen is happy and proud,
Cluck cluck, cluck-cluck, clucking away.

9. Little Bird

One little bird with lovely feathers blue. *(Hold up first finger)*
Sat beside another one. Then there were two. *(Hold up second finger)*
Two little birds singing in the tree.
Another came to join them. Then there were three. *(Hold up third finger)*
Three little birds, wishing there were more.
Along came another bird. Then there were four. *(Hold up fourth finger)*
Four little birds, glad to be alive.
Found a lonely friend. Then there were five. *(Hold up thumb)*
Five little birds just as happy as can be.
Five little birds singing songs for you and me.

10. Mrs. Pigeon

Mrs. Peck Pigeon
is pecking for bread.
Bob-bob-bob. *(Bob head up and down)*
Goes her little round head.
Tame as a kitty cat,
In the street.
Step, step, step, *(Take three steps)*
Go her little red feet.
With her little red feet, *(Point to feet)*
And her little round head, *(Point to head)*
Mrs. Peck Pigeon
Goes pecking for bread.

11. White Swan

Come, pretty swan. *(Thumb is swan's head--closed fingers are body)*
Swimming over the lake. *(Move your hands to make the swan swim along)*
I've brought you some bread crumbs.
And small bits of cake.
   (Make the swan's head dip down into the water and up again as it eats)

 Take care, pretty swan!
Swim away! Swim away! *(Move your arm quickly to make the swan swim away)*
There's a great hungry crocodile
Coming this way. *(Make crocodile motions, with jaws opening and closing)*
Snip, snap! go his jaws.
He is frightful to see.
But he'll never catch you! *(Point outward)*
And he'll never catch me! *(Point to yourself)*

12. Ten Little Ducklings

Ten little ducklings. *(Move hands back and forth in waddling motion)*
Dash, dash, dash!
Jumped in the duck pond. *(Motion of jumping)*
Splash, splash, splash!
When the mother called them,
"Quack, quack, quack."
Ten little ducklings
swam right back. *(Motion of swimming)*

13. Alligator Finger Play

Here is the alligator. *(Right hand forms alligator)*
Sitting on a log. *(Right hand on left forearm)*
Down in the pool *(Make horizontal circle of arm)*
He sees a little frog. *(Put hands around eyes like binoculars)*
In goes the alligator. *(Diving motion with hands)*
Round goes the log. *(Forearms go round each other)*
Splash goes the water. *(Hands go up in the air)*
Away swims the frog. *(Swimming motion with hands)*

14. Turtle

There was a little turtle who lived in a box. *(Crouch down and pretend to have shell on back)*
He snapped at a mosquito, he snapped at a flea. *(Snapping actions)*
He snapped at a minnow, and he snapped at me.
He caught a mosquito, he caught the flea. *(Pretend to catch)*
He caught the minnow, but he didn't catch me.

15. Froggies

This little froggie broke his toe. *(Point to one finger at a time)*
This little froggie said, "Oh, oh, oh".
This little froggie laughed and was glad.
This little froggie cried and was sad.
This little froggie did just what he should.
Hopped straight to his mother as fast as he could. *(Hop fingers away).*

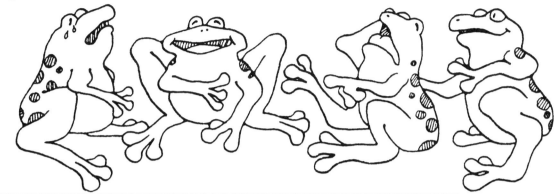

16. Little Green Frog

"Gung, gung" went the lit-tle green frog one day.
"Gung, gung" went the lit-tle green frog.
"Gung, gung" went the lit-tle green frog one day.
And his eyes went "aah, aah, gung."

BURP!

17. Boa Constrictor

There is a boa constrictor and here he comes.
Oh, no! He's got my toe.
Oh, gee! He's got my knee.
Oh, my! He's got my thigh.
Oh, fiddle! He's got my middle.
Oh, darn! He's got my arm.
Oh, heck! He's got my neck.
Oh, dread! He's got my head *(gulp)*

18. Snail

This is a favorite game with very little children. For large numbers, each verse may be repeated as needed to complete the winding or unwinding of the line. The players all stand in a line holding hands and saying the first verse. They wind up in a spiral, following the leader, who walks in a circle, which grows ever smaller until all are wound up, still holding hands. The leader then turns and unwinds, until all are again in one long line.

Hand in hand you see us well.
Creep like a snail into his shell.
Ever nearer, ever nearer,
Ever closer, ever closer,
Very snug indeed you dwell,
Snail, within your tiny shell.

Hand in hand you see us well.
Creep like a snail out of his shell.
Ever farther, ever farther,
Ever wider, ever wider.
Who'd have thought this tiny shell
Could have held us all so well.

19. Little Toad

I am a little toad,
Hopping down the road. *(Make fingers hop in time to verse)*
Just listen to my song.
I sleep all winter long. *(Palms together at side of head)*
When spring comes, I peep out. *(Peep behind hands)*
And then I jump about. *(Make arms jump)*
And now I catch a fly. *(Clap hands)*
And now I wink my eye. *(Wink one eye)*
And now and then I hop. *(Make hands hop)*
And now and then I stop. *(Fold hands)*

20. Body Plays

a. Elephant

His name is Elmer Elephant.
His lip and trunk are one.
And when I went to pick him up,
I found he weighed a ton.

b. Lion

Lion paced the jungle floor.
And then let out a mighty roar.
"My stomach is empty. What can I do?"
"I know what--I'll nibble on you!"

c. Kangaroo

Kangaroo babies
Have more fun than any others.
They jump right out,
While hopping with their mothers.

d. Dog

Dog chases his tail.
Till he's ready to sleep.
Then curls right up
In a little heap.

21. Going On A Bear Hunt
Or Lion Hunt Or Whatever Hunt

Teacher: We're going on a bear hunt
Children: We're going on a bear hunt.
Teacher: We're not afraid.
Children: We're not afraid.
Teacher: Are we?
Children: Are we?
Teacher: No.
Children: No.

Teacher talks and teacher and children act out motions. *(For example: "Let's take off our pajamas, and put on our pants, our shirt, boots, hat, flashlight, binoculars, cameras, misc.")*

Teacher: Here we go. *(Repeat first verse--"We're going on a bear hunt, etc.")*

Teacher: Off we go through the jungle and look over there, there is a river and we can't go around it and we can't fly over it. We must swim it. Let's go. *(Act out swimming motion)*
Now we're on the other side. Let's shake off and keep going. Look! There is some very tall grass; we must go through it *(Make swishing sound and motion by rubbing hands together)* Oh, Oh! There is a tall tree and we can't go under it and we can't go around it and we can't go over it so we must climb it. *(Pretend to be climbing a tree)*
Now we're at the top. Let's look around. Let's take out our binoculars and see if we see a bear. No, no bears around here. Let's go down the tree and keep going.
Oh my! There is a big mud puddle here and we can't go over it and it's too big to go around it so we must go through it. *(Make mud sound by inflating cheeks and pushing them in with fingers)* Let's sit down now and take a break for lunch. *(Pretend to be eating and chat with children)*
Time to get going again. Start walking again. Uh-oh. There is a herd of elephants over there and we don't want to bother them, so let's tiptoe quietly past them. *(Tiptoe in place or in sitting position)*
Whew, we did it.
Let's keep walking and walking. Oh no, a bridge. But we can go over it. *(Beat on chest for sound of walking over bridge)*
Now let's take a look in that cave over there. First let's get out our flashlight and look around. Hummmmmmmmmmmm.

71

YIKES, there's a BEAR! *(Now repeat actions backwards in triple time as if running away from the bear. For example: "Let's run out of the cave, over the bridge, tiptoe past the elephants, etc.")*

Teacher: Whew, we're home. Let's slam the door.
Teacher: We went on a bear hunt.
Children: We went on a bear hunt.
Teacher: We weren't afraid.
Children: We weren't afraid.
Teacher: Were we?
Children: Were we?
Teacher: No.
Children: No.

22. Five little Monkeys Jumping on the Bed

Five little monkeys jumping on the bed.
One fell off and cracked his head.
Mommy called the doctor and the doctor said,
"No more monkeys jumping on the bed."
Four little monkeys jumping on the bed.
One fell off and cracked his head.
Mommy called the doctor and the doctor said,
"No more monkeys jumping on the bed."

(Continue with three, two and one.)
Last verse says;
One little monkey jumping on the bed.
He fell off and broke his head.
Mommy called the doctor and the doctor said,
"No more monkeys jumping on the bed."
Then there were no more monkeys jumping on the bed.

23. Monkey See And Monkey Do

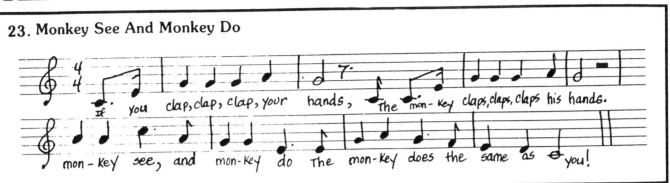

If you clap, clap, clap, your hands, The mon-key claps, claps, claps his hands.
mon-key see, and mon-key do The mon-key does the same as you!

2. If you tap, tap, tap your head…
3. If you stamp, stamp, stamp your feet…
4. If you bend, bend, bend your knees…
5. If you turn, turn, turn around…
6. If you hop, hop, hop in place…
7. If you sing this very loud…
8. If you sing this very soft…
9. If you sing this very slow…
10. If you sing this very fast…

24. Five Little Monkeys Swinging From A Tree

Five little monkeys swinging from a tree.
Teasing Mr. Crocodile, "You can't catch me."*(Swing finger as if teasing)*
Along came Mr. Crocodile quietly as can be. *(Arm becomes the crocodile)*
Then SNAP. *(Two arms together as if crocodile's mouth)*
Then there were four little monkeys swinging from a tree.
Teasing Mr. Crocodile, "You can't catch me."
(Continue with 3. 2. 1 and then the last line says:)

Then there were no more monkeys swinging from the tree.

25. Elephant and Telephone *(Use with older children)*

Once there was an elephant
Who tried to use the telephant.

No, no, I mean the telephone.

How could it be, he got his trunk
Entangled in the telephunk.

The more he tried to get it free,
The louder buzzed the telephee.

Dear me, I think I'd better drop my song
Of elephop and telephong.

The more I try to say it right
The more I seem to get it wrong!

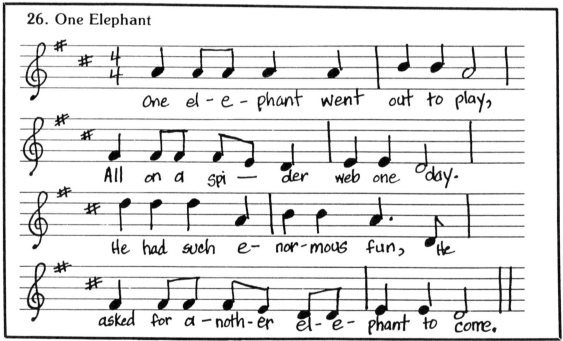

26. One Elephant

One el-e-phant went out to play,
All on a spi — der web one day.
He had such e-nor-mous fun,
He asked for a-noth-er el-e-phant to come.

2. Two elephants went out to play . . .
3. Three elephants . . .
4. Four elephants . . .
5. Five elephants . . .
6. Six elephants . . .
7. Seven elephants . . .
8. Eight elephants . . .
9. Nine elephants . . .
10. Ten elephants went out to play,
All on a spider web one day.
They had such enormous fun,
They didn't ask another elephant to come.

-74-

26. The Elephant

The elephant has a trunk for a nose. *(Pretend an arm is the trunk)*
And up and down is the way it goes. *(Move arm up and down)*
He wears such a saggy, baggy hide.
Do you think two elephants would fit inside?

27. The Elephant's Trunk

The elephant has a great big trunk *(Pretend an arm is the trunk)*
That goes swinging, swinging so, *(Swing trunk)*
He has tiny, tiny eyes that show him where to go. *(Point to eyes)*
His huge long ears go flapping, flapping up and down. *(Pretend hands are ears)*
His great feet go stomping, stomping on the ground. *(Stamp feet)*

28. Teddy Bear

Teddy Bear, Teddy Bear, turn around.
Teddy Bear, Teddy Bear, touch the ground.
Teddy Bear, Teddy Bear, show your shoe.
Teddy Bear, Teddy Bear, that will do!

Teddy Bear, Teddy Bear, go upstairs.
Teddy Bear, Teddy Bear, say your prayers.
Teddy Bear, Teddy Bear, switch off the light.
Teddy Bear, Teddy Bear, say good-night.

(Pantomime the words)

29. Five little Polar Bears

Five little polar bears *(Hold up one hand)*
Playing on the shore.
One fell in the water.
And then there were four. *(Put down one finger)*

Four little polar bears
Swimming out to sea.
One got lost.
And then there were three.

Three little polar bears said
"What shall we do?"
One climbed an iceberg.
Then there were two.

Two little polar bears
Playing in the sun.
One went for food
Then there was one.

One little polar bear
Didn't want to stay.
He said "I'm lonesome,"
And swam far away.

30. This Little Bear

This little bear has a fur suit. *(Thumb)*
This little bear acts very cute. *(Pointer finger)*
This little bear is bold and cross. *(Middle finger)*
This little bear says, "You're not boss." *(Ring finger)*
This little bear likes bacon and honey. *(Little finger)*
But he can't buy them, he has no money!

31. Animal Poem

I'm a little kitty.
I love to tippy toe.
Won't you do it with me?
Ready now, let's go.
I'm a little rabbit.
I love to hop, hop, hop.
Come on, and do it with me.
It's fun; we'll never stop.
I'm a great big elephant.
I take big steps so slow.
I'd love to have you join me.
Ready now, let's go.
I'm a little dog.
Who loves to run and run.
If you would do it with me,
We could have such fun.

32. Kitty

Warm kitty, soft kitty, little ball of furr.
Sleepy kitty, happy kitty, purr, purr, purrrrrrrrrr.

33. Three Little Kittens *(Traditional Tune)*

Three little kittens, they lost their mittens, and they began to cry.
Mee-ow, mee-ow, me oh my.
What! Lost your mittens? You naughty kittens. Now you shall have no pie.
Mee-ow, mee-ow, me oh my.
You found your mittens? You good little kittens. Now you shall have some pie.
Mee-ow, mee-ow, me oh my.

34. Kitty *(Tune: "Bingo")*

I have a cat. She's ver-y shy.
But she comes when I call K-I-T-T-Y!
K-I-T-T-Y!
K-I-T-T-Y!
K-I-T-T-Y!
and KIT-TY was her name-o.

36. Pussy-Cat

Pussy-cat, pussy-cat, where've you been?
I've been to London to visit the Queen.
Pussy-cat, pussy-cat, what'd you do there?
I frightened a little mouse under a chair.

37. Mrs. Kitty's Dinner

Mrs. Kitty, sleek and fat, *(Put thumb up with fingers folded on right hand)*
With her kittens four. *(Hold up four fingers on right hand)*
Went to sleep upon the mat *(Make a fist)*
By the kitchen door.

Mrs. Kitty heard a noise.
Up she jumped in glee. *(Thumb up on right hand)*
"Kittens, maybe that's a mouse? *(All five fingers on right hand up)*
Let's go and see!"

Creeping, creeping, creeping on. *(Slowly sneaking with five fingers on floor)*
Silently they stole.
But the little mouse had gone *(Mouse is thumb on left hand)*
Back into his hole.

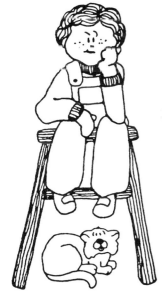

38. A Kitten

A kitten is fast asleep under the chair. *(Thumb under hands)*
And Donald can't find her.
He's looked everywhere. *(Fingers circling eyes to look)*
Under the table. *(Peek under one hand)*
And under the bed *(Peek under other hand)*
He looked in the corner, and then Donald said,
"Come kitty, come kitty, this milk is for you." *(Curve hands for dish)*
And out came kitty, calling "mew, mew, mew".

39. Animal Cracker Rhythmics *(Act Out)*

a. Bunnies in the meadow, hop, hop, hop!
   Bunnies in the clover, stop, stop, stop!
   Here comes a man with his dog and a gun!
   Watch out bunnies. Run, run, run!

b. Reach up real high, stretch up tall.
   Let's be giraffes, they have a ball.
   Picnicking on leaves, eating and chewing,
   Watching what all of the rest are doing.

c. Come on. We're lions. Crouch and creep.
   Slowly, softly, now roarRRR and leap.
   And leap and roarRRR all over the floor.
   Come on, it's fun. Let's do it once more.

d. Here's a vain fellow who is quite grand.
   Opening and closing his tail like a fan.
   Preening and posing and strutting about.
   Now we're peacocks with feathers spread out.

e. I'm a little dog,
   Who loves to run and run.
   If you would do it with me,
   We could have such fun.

   (These are perfect for acting out)

40. Once I Saw A Bunny

Once I saw a bunny. *(Put pointer and middle finger up on right hand)*
And a green cabbage head. *(Make a cabbage head with your left fist)*
"I think I'll have some cabbage,"
The little bunny said. *(Make the bunny hop to the cabbage)*
So he nibbled and he nibbled,
    (Make nibbling motions with the fingers of your right hand)
Then he pricked his ears to say *(Straighten up the two fingers that are the bunny's ears)*
"Now I think it's time
I should be hopping on my way." *(Let the bunny hop away)*

41. I Wish I Were

I wish I were a rabbit, a rabbit, a rabbit.
I wish I were a rabbit. I know what I would do.
I'd go like this--hop-hop, hop-hop!
I'd go like this--hop-hop, hop-hop!
I'd go like this--hop-hop, hop-hop!
And that's what I would do.

Make up some words of your own. Pretend you are a bird, a galloping horse, a butterfly, or anything you like.

42. Not Say A Single Word

We'll hop, hop, hop like a bunny. *(Make hopping motion with hands)*
And run, run, run like a dog. *(Make running motion with fingers)*
We'll walk, walk, walk like an elephant. *(Make walking motion with arms)*
And jump, jump, jump like a frog. *(Make jumping motions with arms)*
We'll swim, swim, swim like a goldfish. *(Make swimming motion with hand)*
And fly, fly, fly like a bird. *(Make flying motion with arms)*
We'll sit right down and fold our hands. *(Fold hands in lap)*
And not say a single word!

43. Bunny

Here is a bunny with ears so funny. *(Right fist with two fingers raised)*
And here is his home in the ground. *(Cup left hand)*
When a noise he hears, he pricks up his ears.
And he jumps to his home in the ground. *(Right two fingers dive into cupped left hand)*

44. Hot Dog

I had a little puppy. He didn't have a tail.
He wasn't very chubby. He was skinny as a rail.
He'll always be a puppy. He'll never be a hound.
They sell him at the butcher shop for ninety cents a pound.
Bow wow wow wow wow wow wow. Hot dog.

45. Bingo *(Traditional Tune)*

There was a farmer had a dog
And Bin-go was his name-o.
B-I-N-G-O,
B-I-N-G-O,
B-I-N-G-O,
And Bin-go was his name-o.

2. ...*(Clap)*-I-N-G-O...
3. ...*(X)*-*(X)*-N-G-O...
4. ...*(X)*-*(X)*-*(X)*-G-O...
5. ...*(X)*-*(X)*-*(X)*-*(X)*-O...
6. ...*(X)*-*(X)*-*(X)*-*(X)*-*(X)*...

46. Fish Alive

One, two, three, four, five. I caught a fish alive.
Six, seven, eight, nine, ten. I let him go again.
Why did you let him go? 'Cuz he bit my finger so.
Which one did he bite? The little one on the right.

47. Five Little Fishes

Five little fishes swimming in a pool. *(Wiggle five fingers)*
First one said, "The pool is cool". *(Wrap arms around body)*
Second one said, "The pool is deep". *(Voice deep)*
Third one said, "I want to sleep". *(Hand dives and dips)*
Fourth one said, "Let's take a dip". *(Swimming motion)*
Fifth one said, "I spy a ship". *(Peer out under hand)*
Fisherman boat comes, *(Fingers form V and move away from body*
Line goes ker-splash, *(Pantomime throwing fishing line)*
Away the five little fishies dash. *(Wiggle five fingers away)*

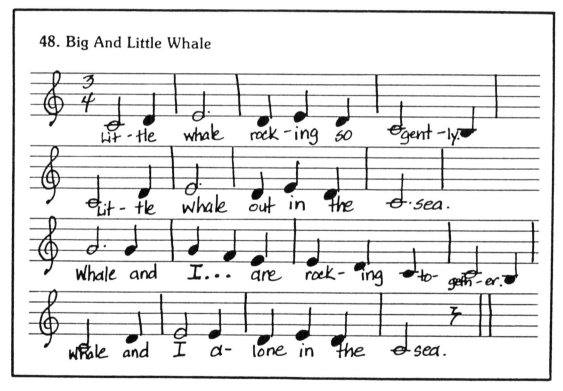

48. Big And Little Whale

Lit-tle whale rock-ing so gent-ly.

Lit-tle whale out in the sea.

Whale and I... are rock-ing to-geth-er.

Whale and I a-lone in the sea.

Great big whale swimming so strongly.
Great big whale out in the sea.
Whale and I...are swimming together.
Whale and I alone in the sea.

49. Did You Feed My Cow?

Teacher says first line and children answer the question.

T: Did you feed my cow?
C: Yes, sir.
T: What did you feed her?
C: Corn and hay.
T: What did you feed her?
C: Corn and hay.
T: Did you milk my cow?
C: Yes, sir.
T: Would you show me how?
C: Yes, sir.
T: How did you milk her?
C: Squish, squish, squish *(Motion like milking udders)*
T: How did you milk her?
C: Squish, squish, squish.
T: Did my cow give milk?
C: Yes, sir.
T: Was it smooth as silk?
C: Yes, sir.
T: How did it taste?
C: MMMMMMMgood.
T: How did it taste?
C: MMMMMMgood.
T: Did my cow want to play?
C: Yes, sir.
T: Did my cow run away?
C: Yes, sir.
T: How did she run?
C: Plop, plop, plop! *(Use plopping motion with hands)*
T: How did she run?
C: Plop, plop, plop.

50. The Mice

Five little mice on the pantry floor.
Seeking for bread crumbs or something more.
Five little mice on the shelf up high.
Feasting so daintily on a pie.
But the big round eyes of the wise old cat,
See what the five little mice are at.
Quickly she jumps! But the mice run away.
And hide in their snug little holes all day.

51. Five Little Mice *(Tune: "Three Little Ducks That I Once Knew)*

Five little mice came out to play.
Gathering crumbs along the way.
Out came pussycat sleek and fat.
Four little mice go scampering back.

Fingerplay:
Fingers on right hand in running movement.
Left hand is pussycat who catches one
mouse. This may be played as a game, using
five children as mice and one as cat.

52. Hickory, Dickory Dock

Hick-o-ry, dick-o-ry dock. *(Hands in praying position, rock back and forth)*
The mouse ran up the clock.
The clock struck one. *(Clap hands above head)*
The mouse ran down. *(Wiggle fingers downward)*
Hick-o-ry, dick-o-ry dock. *(Praying hands position, rock back and forth)*
The clock struck two. *(Clap, clap)*
The mouse said "Boo!"
The clock struck three. *(Clap, clap, clap)*
The mouse said "Whee!"
The clock struck four. *(Clap, clap, clap, clap)*
The mouse said "No more!"

53. Mice

Five little mice on the pantry floor.
   (Hold up five fingers)
This little mouse peeked behind the door.
   (Bend down little finger)
This little mouse nibbled at the cake.
   (Bend down ring finger)
This little mouse took a bit of cheese.
   (Bend down pointer finger)
This little mouse heard the kitten sneeze.
   (Bend thumb)
"Ah Choo!" sneezed the kitten and "squeak!" they cried.
As they found a hole and ran inside.
   (Mice running motions with fingers and hide hands behind back)

54. Baby Mice

Where are the baby mice?
Squeak, squeak, squeak! *(Make fist and hide it behind you)*
I cannot see them.
Peek, peek, peek! *(Show fist and extend it)*
Here they come out of their hole in the wall.
One, two, three, four, five and this is all! *(Show one finger at a time)*

55. This Little Cow

This little cow eats grass. *(Hold up one hand, fingers erect, bend down one finger)*
This little cow eats hay. *(Bend down another finger)*
This little cow drinks water. *(Bend down another finger)*
And this little cow runs away. *(Bend down another finger)*
But this little cow lies and sleeps all day. *(Bend down another finger)*

56. Old MacDonald *(Traditional Tune)*

Old MacDonald had a farm, ee, ii, ee, ii, oo.
And on his farm he had a cow, ee, ii, ee, ii, oo.
With a "moo moo" here,
And a "moo moo" there,
Here a "moo",
There a "moo",
Everywhere a "moo moo".
Old MacDonald had a farm, ee, ii, ee, ii, ooooooooooo.

Pig, "oink oink"; chick, "cluck cluck"; horse, "neigh neigh"; sheep, "baa baa"; dog, "arf, arf"; turkey, "gobble, gobble"; cats, "meow meow"; ducks, "quack quack".

57. This Little Pig

This little pig went to market.
 (Point to one finger at a time)
This little pig stayed home.
This little pig had roast beef.
This little pig had none.
This little pig cried "Wee, wee, weee".
And ran all the way home.

58. Piggies

"Its time for my piggies to get to bed."
The nice big mother piggie said.
"Now I must count them up to see
If all my piggies came back to me.
One little piggy, two little piggies,
Three little piggies dear.
Four little piggies, five little piggies.
Yes, they all are here.
They're the dearest little piggies alive.
One, two, three, four, five."

59. Eight Pigs

Two mother pigs lived in a pen. *(Thumbs)*
Each had four babies and that made ten. *(Fingers of both hands)*
These four babies were black and white. *(Fingers of one hand)*
These four babies were black as night. *(Fingers of the other hand)*
All eight babies loved to play. *(Wiggle fingers)*
And they rolled and they rolled in the mud all day. *(Roll hands)*

60. The Five E-Nor-Mous Dinosaurs *(Fingerplay)*

Five E-Nor-Mous dinosaurs *(Arms extend to sides)*
Shouting out a roar. *(Cup hands over mouth like megaphone)*
Along came an alligator. *(Move hand in wavy motion)*
Then there were four. *(Hold up four fingers)*
Four E-Nor-Mous dinosaurs *(Extend arms to sides)*
Sitting in a tree.
'Til the wind blew by. *(Sweep hands across body)*
Then there were three. *(Hold up three fingers)*
Three E-Nor-Mous dinosaurs *(Extend arms to sides)*
Were taken to the zoo.
'Til one got away.
Then there were two. *(Hold up two fingers)*
Two E-Nor-Mous dinosaurs
Were having such fun.
'Til a volcano blew up. *(Push both arms above head)*
Then there was one. *(Hold up one finger)*
One E-Nor-Mous dinosaur *(Extend arms to sides)*
He must have weighed a ton.
'Til the lakes dried up.
Then there were none!

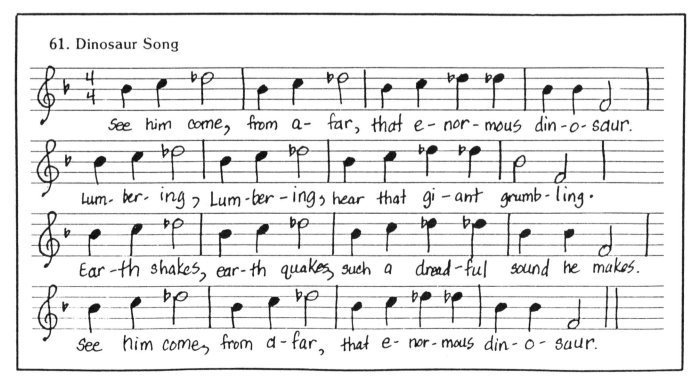

61. Dinosaur Song

See him come, from a-far, that e-nor-mous din-o-saur.

Lum-ber-ing, Lum-ber-ing, hear that gi-ant grumb-ling.

Ear-th shakes, ear-th quakes, such a dread-ful sound he makes.

See him come, from a-far, that e-nor-mous din-o-saur.

62. The Stegasaurus

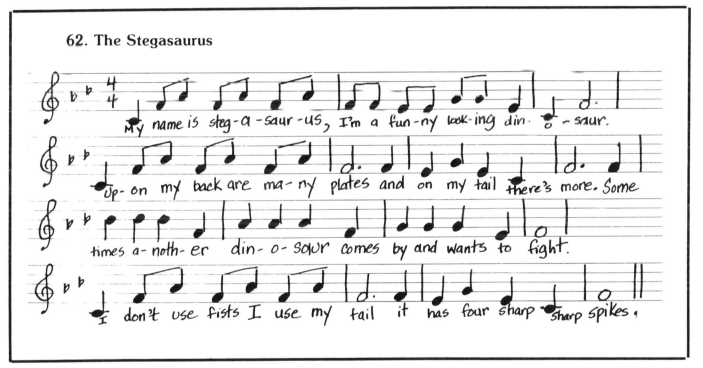

My name is steg-a-saur-us, I'm a fun-ny look-ing din-o-saur.

Up-on my back are ma-ny plates and on my tail there's more. Some

times a-noth-er din-o-saur comes by and wants to fight.

I don't use fists I use my tail it has four sharp sharp spikes,

63. Pop! Goes The Weasel *(Traditional Tune)*

All around the cob-bler's bench, *(Make circle in air with finger)*
The mon-key chased the wea-sel. *(Chase one hand with the other hand)*
The mon-key thought 'twas all in fun. *(Hands at either side of head--rock sideways)*
Pop! *(Clap)* goes the wea-sel.

Action suggestions:
1. Roll hands while singing, clap on "pop".
2. Walk in circle, fall on "pop".

64. Seals

The seals all slap their shining flips. *(Put hands under arms and flap arms)*
And bounce a ball on their nosey tips. *(Point to nose)*
And beat a drum and catch a bar. *(Beat a drum)*
And wriggle how pleased they are. *(Wriggle)*

65. This Little Leopard

This little leopard is very wild. *(Thumb)*
This little leopard is a loving child. *(Pointer finger)*
This little leopard has some big black spots. *(Middle finger)*
This little leopard has small black dots. *(Ring finger)*
This little leopard likes to prowl and smell. *(Little finger)*
But his teeth are too small to bite very well.

66. The Yellow Giraffe

The yellow giraffe is tall as can be. *(Put hands up high)*
His lunch is a bunch of leaves off a tree. *(Put arm up for tree branches)*
He has a very long neck and his legs are long too. *(Point to neck and legs)*
And he can run faster than his friends in the zoo. *(Run in place)*

67. The Funny Fat Walrus

The funny fat walrus sits in the sea.
Where the weather is freezing and cold as can be.
  (Put hands on arms and shiver)
His whiskers are droopy and his tusks are white.
And he doesn't do much but sit day and night.

68. The Brown Kangaroo

The brown kangaroo is very funny.
She leaps and runs and hops like a bunny. *(Hop)*
And on her stomach is a pocket so wide.
  (Put hand on stomach like a pocket)
Her baby can jump in and go for a ride.
  (Have other hand jump into pocket)

69. The Kangaroo

Said the kind kangaroo,
"What can I do? *(Hold out hands with palms up)*
If I had a cradle, I'd rock it. *(Cup hands and move back and forth)*
But my baby is small.
So I think after all,
I'll carry him 'round in my pocket!"
  (Put one hand on stomach for a pocket
and put other hand inside "pocket")*

circus

Each year our school has a unit studying the circus and we have found some of these activities fun to share.

1. Ten Circus Wagons

(Only use this with pictures because it is rather long and the children will enjoy visual clues.)

Ten circus wagons, painted oh so gay.
Came into town with the circus today! *(Hold up ten fingers)*
This one holds a lion.
That gives a big, loud roar! *(Point to thumb)*
This one holds a tiger
Fast asleep upon the floor. *(Pointer finger)*
This one holds a funny seal
That nods to the left and right. *(Middle finger)*
This one holds a zebra
That is striped black and white. *(Ring finger)*
This one holds a camel
With two humps upon his back. *(Little finger)*
This one holds a panther
With a coat so black. *(Thumb of other hand)*
This one holds an elephant
That is drinking from a pail. *(Pointer finger)*
This one holds a monkey
That is swinging by his tail. *(Middle finger)*
This one holds a hippo
With a grin so very wide. *(Ring finger)*
This one holds a leopard
With a gaily spotted hide. *(Little finger)*
Ten circus wagons, painted oh so gay.
Came into town with the circus today. *(Ten fingers)*

2. This Little Clown

This little clown is fat and gay. *(Thumb)*
This little clown does tricks all day. *(Pointer finger)*
This little clown is tall and strong. *(Middle finger)*
This little clown is dancing along. *(Ring Finger)*
This little clown is wee and small. *(Little finger)*
But he can do anything at all!

3. Where Was I?

(Tune: "Big And Little Whale")

I saw clowns
Laughing and tumbling.
Bands were playing.
Big drums went BOOM! *(Clap)*

Acrobats and tightrope walkers
Elephants parading by.
Lions, tigers, horses prancing.
Can you tell me
Where was I?

4. The Zoo

This is the way the elephant goes.
   (Clasp hands together, extend arms, and move them back and forth)
With curly trunk instead of a nose.
The buffalo, all shaggy and fat,
Has two sharp horns in place of a hat.
The hippo with his mouth so wide.
Lets you see what is inside.
   (Hands together and open and close them to simulate mouth movement)
The wiggly snake upon the ground,
Crawls along without a sound.
   (Weave hands back and forth)
But monkey see and monkey do
Is the funniest animal in the zoo.
   (Place thumbs in ears and wiggle hands)

5. One, One. The Zoo Is Lots Of Fun

One, one. The zoo is lots of fun!
   (Hold up hands with fingers extended;
   bend down one finger as you say each line)

Two, two. See a kangaroo.
Three, three. See a chimpanzee.
Four, four. Hear the lions roar.
Five, five. Watch the seals dive.
Six, six. There's a monkey doing tricks.
Seven, seven. Elephants eleven.
Eight, eight. A tiger and his mate.
Nine, nine. Penguins in a line.
Ten, ten. I want to come again.

creative dramatics

Young children love creative dramatics but often are a bit shy getting started. The following ideas helped us successfully launch drama into our program. Try them!

1. Mulberry Bush *(Traditional Tune)*

Sing the song:

Here we go 'round the mulberry bush,
The mulberry bush,
The mulberry bush.
Here we go 'round the mulberry bush,
So early in the morning.

This is the way we....and then act something out for the children to guess. *(For example: brush your teeth)* Then let the children have turns pantomiming out morning activities. *(Other examples: comb hair, take shower, make bed, get dressed, eat breakfast, etc.)*

2. Lassie *(Traditional Tune)*

Sing the song "Did You Ever See A Lassie/Laddie?". Have one child in the middle of the circle act out something, and ask the other children to copy the action.

Did you ever see a lassie/laddie,
A lassie/laddie,
A lassie/laddie,
Did you ever see a lassie/laddie
Go this way and that?
Go this way and that way,
Go this way and that way,
Did you ever see a lassie/laddie
Go this way and that.

3. Body Plays *(Moving Stories)*

You are suggesting these images to children as they close their eyes and visualize them. They can also be used as yoga.

a. Strangeness-Joyfulness *(Opposites)*

You are in a strange room.
You do not recognize where you are.
There are strange things in the room.

You are in a wonderful place.
It is where you have always wanted to be.
You feel very good inside.
All is warm, and safe, and cozy.

b. Hot-Cold *(Opposites)*

You are in a cold room.
There is no fire or heat.
You want a jacket.
You look for one.
You can't find a coat.
You are freezing.

You are in a warm room.
The windows are closed and locked.
The heater is on.
It cannot be turned off.
You are very warm and are sweating.
It is daytime.
The sun will not stop shining.

4. Let's Pretend

Before you read a verse, ask a child how he would make the motion which the verse suggests. For example: "How do you ride a pony?" Ask him how the pony would fall down. Emphasize the fact that the child must stop at the end of each verse.

Oh, let's pretend! Yes, let's pretend.
That we are something new.
Let's pretend we're lots of things.
And see what we can do.

(David) is a cowboy,
Riding up a hill. *(Ride pony)*
Until his pony stumbles
And David takes a spill. *(Fall down)*

(Jeanne) is an autumn leaf.
She twirls and twirls around.
  (Dance with many turns)
She twists and turns and twirls again.
And tumbles to the ground. *(Fall down)*

(Kathy) is a candle straight.
Too bad! She got too hot.
  (Stand tall and straight)
She's bending almost double.
Something like a knot. *(Bend way over)*

(Kevin) is an airplane.
Flying high and grand.
    (Extend arms and glide around room)
Until he sees an airport,
Where he has to land.
    (Bend knees until extended arms touch
floor)

(Sally) is a firefly.
Flitting in the night.
    (Dance with jerky motions)
Until the morning comes
And she puts out her light.
    (Kneel down and curl up)

(Ken) is a snowman.
Who smiles and looks around.
    (Stand still and smile)
Until the sun smiles back at him.
And he melts to the the ground.
    (Gradually kneel as if melting)

What else can you pretend?
What do other people do?
If you will act it out,
I'll try to do it, too.

The ideas for body imagery are endless. Look at animals, insects, machines, the environment, to see how they move. (Experience different textures to see how they feel)

5. Make Up Stories

The teacher begins a story and lets the children continue with it. For example: you might begin by saying "It is the week before Thanksgiving. As Farmer Brown was feeding the turkeys, he exclaimed, 'There is the turkey I am going to kill for our Thanksgiving dinner.' Now this turkey didn't think much of this idea so he...."

Or, A little girl was going for a walk with her dog and all of a sudden....
Or, Suzie had a very frightening dream last night. It was about....

(This is a good way for children to open up about some of their own fears or bad dreams.)

6. The Classics

Children love to hear the classics over and over again, such as Little Red Riding Hood, The Three Bears, etc.

When they are really familiar with these stories, give them a chance to participate by stopping before the most familiar lines. Some possibilities are (1) In Little Red Riding Hood, "Why Grandma, what big eyes you have!" Then let the children answer "The better to see you with, my dear." (2) In Goldilocks and the Three Bears, "She tasted the porridge in the little tiny bowl." The children say "and this one was too cold, too hot, or this one is just right."

7. Magic Blankets

An old baby blanket or towel makes an excellent prop for creative dramatics. First demonstrate a possible use, such as a Superman cape. Then ask the children if they can think of possible uses. Some examples might be bridal veil, table cloth, toreador capes, skirts, baby blankets, etc.

8. Magic Wand

Magic wand can be a dowel covered with foil or a magic hat *(any kind of witch's pointed hat)* or a magic cape *(black is best)*. Any of these props can be used for this game. Have the children one at a time play the wizard. The other children must be what the wizard wants them to be. For example: the wizard stands up and waves the magic wand and says some magic words previously agreed upon and turns everyone into a snake. The group must act out snake actions. The wizard then says "stop" and its time for another person to be a wizard.

9. Machine Game

Explain to children that they are going to make their bodies become machines. They will act out one particular machine while the others try to guess what they are. *(For example: robots, washing machines, sirens, pogo sticks, record players, T.V., cars, trains, planes, etc.)*

The teacher should be first to pantomime the machine, and then turn it over to volunteer one at a time.

10. Mirror Game

The teacher stands in front of a mirror and shows the children how mirrors do whatever she does. Let the children experiment.

Now the teacher makes movements to the children and the children must "mirror" back what the teacher is doing. Let the children be the leader one at a time.

11. Balloon Pop

Do this activity in an open, large space. Have the children hold hands and form a circle. Explain the action of a balloon, stressing that the balloon get bigger *(expands)* as we blow air into it.

Have the children huddle close together with hands held. Pretend that someone is blowing air into our balloon and it is getting bigger and bigger. As this happens, make the circle bigger and bigger by moving backward. When the tension on the hands becomes great, everyone falls down and says "boom", as if the balloon popped.

12. Follow The Leader

Have children form a line in back of teacher. Lead them around the room, weaving different patterns, and verbally directing them while walking.

Change movements. Gallop, skip, hop, run, walk on heels, walk with still legs, walk with jelly legs, walk backwards, crawl, etc. Then allow a child to be leader.

13. Balloon Act

Let children pretend that they each have a balloon in their hands.

1. Let children sit on the floor. Ask them to pretend that they have a bubble in their hands and they cannot let it burst. Then ask them to stand up very gently and be sure not to let their bubbles drop to the floor.

2. Pretend the balloons are space ships, clouds, sun rising and setting, etc., and ask them to execute these improvisations .

3. Finally, put the balloons away, being very careful not to break them.

14. Musical Housework

Play some soft music and ask the children to play act various things that their moms and dads do around the house. This could be ironing, washing dishes, hammering a nail, cooking, mowing the lawn, etc. When the leader claps his hands or gives another clue, everyone must think of another thing mother does. Then this action is acted out. An alternative might be to have one child act one of these actions out and have the others guess what she is doing.

15. Noah's Ark

Each animal has a unique way of moving and acting. The teacher should be the leader for the group. Put on some music with a drum-beat, or even clap a certain rhythm or mood. Then you can set the pace for an elephant, monkey, bird, etc. The children can then imitate the leader.

16. Robot Visit

This can help children learn language and movement through drama. A parent puts on a paper bag or some other prop to resemble a robot. Tell the children that the robot was delivered to their school, and that it must have blown a fuse. It does everything wrong. Ask the robot to sit down, and it stands up. The class needs to help fix the robot and must get involved in helping the robot to respond correctly. The class ends up teaching the robot different language concepts, and the children find some special word (perhaps "please") or a button to push to make the robot respond successfully.

17. I Can Be Anything!

I'm a little squirrel.
Scurrying around.
I'm a lazy lizard.
Crawling on the ground.
I'm an airplane.
Zoom, zoom!
I'm drummer boy.
Boom! Boom! Boom!
I'm a furry rabbit.
Hoppity-hop, hop.
I'm the rolling tide.
I never stop.
I'm a bunch of things.
A clock, a toad, a tree.
Come here, everybody.
And watch what I can be!

18. Magic Scarf

The magic scarf goes 'round and 'round.
To pass it quickly you are bound.
If you have it when it stops.
You are "it". *(Child who is "it" can act out a movement and others can guess.)*

19. Oodles of Noodles *(Act Out)*

How would you feel and look if you were an uncooked noodle?
Show me how your fingers would look, your arms, your whole body.
You're cooked and ready to be served.
Show me how you move as you are lifted out of the pot and plopped onto a plate.
Oh! Oh! There's a fork under you. It's lifting you up.
Ooooooooops! You're slipping off.
Now the fork is winding you 'round and 'round.
And suddenly you disappear because you've been eaten up!

20. Movement Phrases

Try to say something without using your voice.
How would you say:

I don't know. *(Shrug shoulders)*
I'm so happy. *(Squeeze self)*
I love you. *(Hug)*
That's terrible. *(Cringe)*
Get out of my way. *(Kick and shove)*
Walk quietly. *(Tiptoe)*
I want to hide. *(Crouch)*
I want that! *(Grab)*
I'm too timid. *(Twist)*
Help! This won't move. *(Tug)*
Don't hit me! *(Jerk)*

21. Creative Expression

See what you can do with just your fingers, hands, arms, and different parts of the body. Now move every part of your body.

Make yourself round.
Make yourself tall, small.
Make yourself very quiet and relaxed.
Blink like a cat.
Crawl like a snake.
Wiggle like a worm.
Be a tin soldier.
Be an astronaut floating in space.
Be a balloon being inflated.
   Be a balloon let go.
   Be a balloon popped
Grow like a flower.
Walk on a tightrope.
Be popcorn being popped.
Be a boat being tossed by the waves.
Be a nail being hammered in a piece of wood.
Be a yo yo.
Be a typewriter.
Be an egg beater.
Be a top.
Gallop like a horse.
Be a monkey swinging from the tree.
Carry something very heavy.
Be a washing machine.
Be a cloud drifting through the sky.
Be a wind-up toy.
Walk like an elephant.
Walk like a spider.

easter

Bunnies, baskets, and eggs are a fun part of every Easter season. Have a good time trying these.

1. Little Peter Rabbit *(Tune: "Glory, Glory, Halleluiah")*

Little Peter Rabbit had a fly upon his nose.
(Hands make rabbit ears, fingers fly away, point to nose)
Little Peter Rabbit had a fly upon his nose.
(Same actions as above)
Little Peter Rabbit had a fly upon his nose.
(Same actions as above)
And he flipped it and he flopped it and it flew away.
(Wave hand over nose, do same as before with other hand, hands together in waving motion)

Leave out word "rabbit" but do motions.
Leave out word "rabbit" and "fly", but do motions.
Leave out word "rabbit" and "fly" and "nose", but do motions.

Suggestion: Other verses to sing:
Little Peter Rabbit had a fly upon his toe.
Little Peter Rabbit had a fly upon his ear.
Little Peter Rabbit had a fly upon his paw.
And he....*(Slap hands together)*

2. Peter Cottontail *(Traditional Tune)*

Here comes Peter Cottontail.
Hopping down the bunny trail.
Hippity, hoppity, Easter's on it's way.
Bringing every girl and boy.
Baskets full of Easter joy.
Things to make your Easter bright and gay.

There'll be jelly beans for Tommy.
Colored eggs for sister Sue.
There's an orchid for your mommy.
And an Easter bonnet too.

Oh, here comes Peter Cottontail.
Hopping down the bunny trail.
Hippity, hoppity, Easter's on it's way.

3. Little Cabin In The Wood *(Traditional Tune)*

Little cabin in the wood.
(Form a peaked roof with fingertips touching)
Little man by the window stood.
(Shade eyes, peer out window)
Saw a rabbit hopping by.
(Middle and forefinger up, make rabbit hop)
Knocking at his door.
(Pantomime knocking)
"Help me! Help me, sir!" he said.
(Wave hands)
Or the hunter will shoot me dead.
(Pantomime shooting shot gun)
"Little rabbit come inside.
(Beckon rabbit)
Happy we will be."
(Pet rabbit)

4. Here Comes Bunny

Here comes bunny-hop, hop, hop.
Two long ears that flop, flop, flop.
Bunny, bunny, won't you stop?
No, I must go-hop, hop, hop.

5. Family Of Rabbits

A family of rabbits lived under a tree.
(Close right hand and hide it under left arm)
A father, a mother and babies three.
(Hold up thumb, then each finger in succession)
Sometimes the bunnies would sleep all day.
(Make fist)
But when night came, they liked to play.
(Wiggle fingers)
Out of the hole they'd go creep, creep, creep.
(Move fingers in creeping motion)
While the birds in the trees were all asleep.
(Rest face on hands, place palms together)
Then the bunnies would scamper about and run.
(Wiggle fingers)
Uphill, downhill, oh, what fun!
(Move fingers vigorously)
But when the mother said, "Its time to rest",
(Hold up middle finger)
Pop! They would hurry
(Clap hands after "pop")
Right back to their nest!
(Hide hand under arm)

6. Five Little Rabbits

Five little rabbits under a log.
(Hold up one hand)
This one said, "Shhh I hear a dog!"
(Point to thumb)
This one said "I see a man!"
(Pointer)
This one said, "Run while you can!"
(Little finger)
A man and his dog went hurrying by.
And you should have seen those rabbits fly!
(Place hand behind back quickly)

7. Bunny In The Wood

There was a bunny who lived in the wood.
He wiggled his ears as a good bunny should.
(Forefinger on either side of head for ears)
He hopped by a squirrel.
(Hold two fingers up and close others on one arm)
He hopped by a tree.
(Take another hop)
He hopped by a duck.
(Take another hop)
And he hopped by me.
(Hop over the opposite fist)
He stared at the squirrel.
He stared at the tree.
He stared at the duck.
But he made faces at me.
(Wiggle nose)

8. Sweet Bunny

There is nothing so sweet as a bunny.
(Hold hands on head for bunny ears)
A dear, little, sweet little bunny.
He can hop on his toes.
(Hop forward)
He can wiggle his nose.
(Wiggle nose)
And his powder puff tail is quite funny.
(Ball formation with hands)

9. Make a Rabbit

Oh, can you make a rabbit
    (Pointer and middle fingers up)
With two ears, so very long?
And let him hop, hop, hop about.
    (Rabbit hops)
On legs so small and strong?
He nibbles, nibbles carrots.

(Insert second finger of left hand for the carrot between the thumb, fourth and fifth fingers of the right hand representing the mouth. Open and close the fingers to imitate nibbling)

For his dinner every day.
As soon as he has had enough,
He scampers away.
    (Rabbit scampers away)

10. Ears So Funny

Here is a bunny with ears so funny.
(Right fist with two fingers raised)
And here is his home in the ground.
(Cup left hand)
When a noise he hears, he pricks up his ears.
And he jumps to his home in the ground.
(Right two fingers dive into cupped left hand)

11. Robbie The Rabbit

Robbie the rabbit is fat, fat, fat.
(Pat stomach)
His soft little paws go pat, pat, pat.
(Pat hands)
His soft little ears go flop, flop, flop.
(Hands on head-flop hands)
And when Robbie runs, he goes hop, hop, hop.
(Hop forward three times)

12. The Little Bunny

This little bunny has two pink eyes.
(Bend down finger)
This little bunny is very wise.
(Bend down second finger)
This little bunny is soft as silk.
(Third finger)
This little bunny is white as milk.
(Fourth finger)
This little bunny nibbles away.
(Bend down thumb)
At cabbage and carrots the live-long day!

MAY AND JUNE

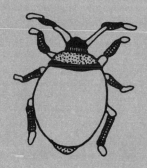

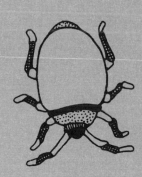

insects

Bet you never thought that insects could be darling. Just read below and see how cute they really are.

1. Eensy Weensy Spider *(Traditional Tune)*

The eensy weensy spider went up the water spout.
(Touch all five fingertips together and move hands in and out as if going up the spout)
Down came the rain.
(fingers represent raindrops)
And washed the spider out.
(Wash away action with hands)
Out came the sun and dried up all the rain.
(Form hands in shape of round sun)
So the eensy weensy spider went
up the spout again.

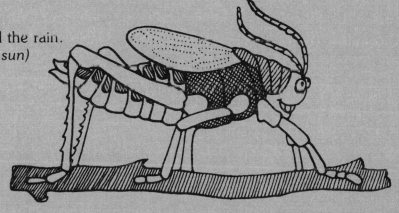

2. Little Grasshopper *(Tune: "Cucaracha")*

Little grasshopper, little grasshopper,
Hop across the grassy land.
Little grasshopper, little grasshopper,
Hop into my open hand.
Little grasshopper, little grasshopper,
Sweet and green as you can be.
Little grasshopper, little grasshopper,
Hop away so safe and free.

3. Bee Hive

Here is the bee hive, where are the bees?
Hidden away where nobody sees. *(Make fist)*
Watch and you'll see them, come out of the hive.
1-2-3-4-5. Buzz-z-z-z *(Flutter fingers)*

4. One, Two, Three, Johnny Caught A Flea

One, two, three. Johnny caught a flea.
Flea died. Johnny cried. Tee- hee-hee.

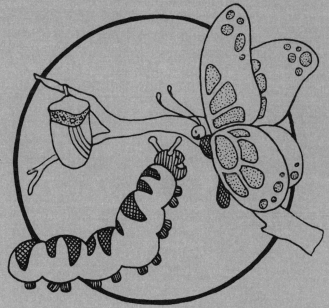

5. The Chrysalis

Here is the chrysalis on a twig on a tree.
(Five fingers extended on left hand acting as the tree and the right hand in ball resting between thumb and pointed finger as the chrysalis)
Something is stirring.
(Hold up to ear)
Let's wait and see.
Something comes out with wings folded tight.
(Thumbs touching each other and fingers folded down)
Now they are spreading all ready for flight.
(Begin to unspread fingers)
It's a beautiful fluttery butterfly.
Away it goes flying—goodbye, goodbye.
(Wave hands as if in flight)

6. Five Busy Bees

Five little busy bees on a day so sunny.
(Hold up all fingers on one hand)
Number one said, "I'd like to make some honey".
(Bend down first finger)
Number two said, "Tell me, where shall it be?"
(Bend down second finger)
Number three said, "In the old honey tree".
(Bend down third finger)
Number four said, Let's gather pollen sweet".
(Bend down fourth finger)
Number five said, Let's take it on our feet".
(Bend down thumb)
Humming their busy little honey-bee song.

7. Caterpillars

"Let's go to sleep", the little caterpillars said.
(Bend ten fingers into palms)
As they tucked themselves into their beds.
They will awaken by and by.
(Slowly unfold and hold up fingers)
And each one will be a lovely butterfly!
(Hands make flying motion)

8. Butterfly Hunting *(Action Verse)*

With a net I go hunting.
To catch a butterfly.
But when he's caught,
I turn him loose.
To fly back into the sky.

9. Wiggly Worm *(Action Verse)*

Wiggly, wiggly,
Wiggly worm.
Wiggles out
Of the earth so firm.
While listening, listening,
Listening low,
Mr. Robin catches
The worm below.

10. Lady Bug

Lady bug, lady bug, fly away home.
Your house in on fire.
Your children are alone.

11. Spider On The Floor

There's a spider on the floor, on the floor,
There's a spider on the floor, on the floor.
Who could ask for any more
Than a spider on the floor
There's a spider on the floor, on the floor

Now the spider's on my leg, on my leg
Oh the spider's on my leg, on my leg
Oh he's really really big!
This old spider on my leg.
There's a spider on my leg, on my leg.

Now the spider's on my stomach, on my stomach
Oh the spider's on my stomach, on my stomach
Oh he's just a dumb old lummok!
This old spider on my stomach.
There's a spider on my stomach, on my stomach.

Now the spider's on my neck, on my neck
Oh the spider's on my neck, on my neck
Oh I'm gonna be a wreck!
I've got a spider on my neck
There's a spider on my neck, on my neck.

Now the spider's on my face, on my face
Oh the spider's on my face, on my face
Oh what a big disgrace!
I've got a spider on my face!
There's a spider on my face, on my face.

Now the spider's on my head, on my head
Oh the spider's on my head, on my head
Oh I wish that I were dead!
I've got a spider on my head!
There's a spider on my head, on my head.

But he jumps off—....

Now there's a spider on the floor, on the floor
There's a spider on the floor, on the floor
Who could ask for any more
Than a spider on the floor
There's a spider on the floor, on the floor.

Children are captivated by leader's facial expressions as leader's hand (the spider)
moves up her body. The children can imitate leader as they make their hand a spider
also, moving up their bodies.

movement activities

These activities are not only fun, but they provide a good learning experience for young children offering an opportunity to learn about spatial relationships, body parts, and kinesthetic mode.

1. Wise Man/Foolish Man
   (Tune: "Glory, Glory, Halleluiah")

The wise man built his house upon the rocks.
   (Act out wise, pounding, rocks, etc.)
The wise man built his house upon the rocks,
   (Building action)
The wise man built his house upon the rocks.
And the rains came tumbling down.
   (Raining action)
The rain came down and the floods came up.
The rain came down and the floods came up.
The rain came down and the floods came up.
And the wise man's house stood firm.

Second verse: Repeat same only with :
   Foolish man built his house upon the sand.
   (make goofy face for foolish)
And the foolish man's house went plop.
   (Plop on floor)

2. The Finger Band *(Tune: "Here We Go 'Round The Mulberry Bush")*

The finger band has come to town.
Come to town, come to town.
The finger band has come to town.
So early in the morning.

2. The finger band can play the drums...
3. flute
4. clarinet
5. trumpet
6. violin
7. trombone
8. piano
9. guitar
10. The finger band has gone away...

Pantomime playing the various instruments.
   (For example: drumming on drums)

3. Looby Loo *(Traditional Tune)*

Here we go looby loo.
Here we go looby light.
Here we go looby loo.
All on a Saturday night.

Put your right foot in.
Put your right foot out.
Give your foot a shake, shake, shake.
And turn yourself about.
Oh....*(Repeat chorus)*

2. Left foot
3. Right hand
4. Left hand
5. Head
6. Whole self

After each verse, join hands and circle around on chorus.

4. She'll Be Comin' 'Round The Mountain (*Traditional Tune*)

She'll be comin' 'round the mountain when she comes, toot toot.
   (*Pantomime pulling rope*)
She'll be comin' 'round the mountain when she comes, toot toot.
She'll be comin' 'round the mountain. She'll be comin' 'round the mountain.
She'll be comin' 'round the mountain when she comes, toot toot.

She'll be drivin' six white horses when she comes, whoa back.
   (*Pull on reins*)

Oh, we'll all go out to meet her when she comes, hi there.
   (*Wave*)

Then we'll kill the old red rooster when she comes, hack, hack.
   (*Make chopping motion*)

And we'll all have chicken and dumplings when she comes, yum yum.
   (*Rub tummy*)

Oh, we'll have to sleep with Grandma when she comes, snore snore.
   (*Make snoring sound*)

5. Rock My Soul (*Traditional Tune*)

Rock my soul in the bosom of Abraham.
Rock my soul in the bosom of Abraham.
Rock my soul in the bosom of Abraham.
Oh, rock my soul.

So high ya can't get over it. (*Put hand over head*)
So low ya can't get under it. (*Hold hand near floor*)
So wide ya can't get around it. (*Hold hands out to the side*)
Gotta go through the door.

6. Skip To My Loo *(Traditional Tune)*

(Skip around in circle)

Flies in the buttermilk.
Shoo fly shoo.
Flies in the buttermilk.
Shoo fly shoo.
Flies in the buttermilk.
Shoo fly shoo.
Skip to my Lou, my darlin'.

(chorus)

Lou, Lou, skip to my Lou.
Lou, Lou, skip to my Lou.
Lou, Lou, skip to my Lou.
Skip to my Lou, my darlin'.

Grab your partner, skip to my Lou.
  (Hold both hands of partner)
Grab your partner, skip to my Lou.
Grab your partner, skip to my Lou.
Skip to my Lou, my darlin'.

(Chorus)

Lost my partner, what'll I do?
  (Walk around pretending to look for partner)
Lost my partner, what'll I do?
Lost my partner, what'll I do?
Skip to my Lou, my darlin'.

(Chorus)

I'll find another one, and it's you.
  (Hold hand with new partner)
I'll find another one, and it's you.
I'll find another one, and it's you.
Skip to my Lou, my darlin'.

7. In And Out The Window *(Traditional Tune)*

Go 'round and 'round the village.
>   *(Children join hands and skip to the right)*

Go 'round and 'round the village.
Go 'round and 'round the village.
As we have done before.

Go in and out the window.
>   *(Everyone joins hands. One child goes in and*
>   *out of joined hands)*

Go in and out the window.
Go in and out the window.
As we have done before.

Now go and pick a partner.
>   *(Children skip to right while one child skips to*
>   *left around the outside circle. When*
>   *verse ends, the child in the circle nearest to*
>   *the outside child becomes the partner)*

Now go and pick a partner.
Now go and pick a partner.
As we have done before.

Now circle with your partner.
>   *(Children stand and clap hands. The partners*
>   *go inside circle and skip in a small circle)*

Now circle with your partner.
Now circle with your partner.
As we have done before.

8. This Old Man *(Traditional Tune)*

This old man, he played one. *(Hold up one finger)*
He played knick-knack on his thumb. *(Tap your thumbs together)*

(Chorus)

Knick-knack, paddy-whack, give the dog a bone.
>   *(clap your hands on your knee, clap your hands together, then hold out one hand*
> *as if you were giving a bone to a dog)*
This old man came rolling home. *(Make a rolling motion with your hands)*

This old man, he played two. *(Hold up two fingers)*
He played knick-knack on his shoe. *(Touch your shoe)*

(Chorus)

This old man, he played three. *(Hold up three fingers)*
He played knick-knack on his knee. *(Touch your knee)*

(Chorus)

This old man, he played four. *(Hold up four fingers)*
He played knick-knack on the floor. *(Touch the floor)*

(Chorus)

This old man, he played five. *(Hold up five fingers)*
He played knick-knack on his hive. *(Touch leg)*

(Chorus)

This old man, he played six. *(Hold up six fingers)*
He played knick-knack on his sticks. *(Tap your pointing fingers together)*

(Chorus)

This old man, he played seven. *(Hold up seven fingers)*
He played knick-knack up in Heaven. *(Point above you)*

(Chorus)

This old man, he played eight. *(Hold up eight fingers)*
He played knick-knack on his plate. *(Touch your head)*

(Chorus)

This old man, he played nine. *(Hold up nine fingers)*
He played knick-knack on his spine. *(Touch your back)*

(Chorus)

This old man, he played ten. *(Hold up ten fingers)*
He played knick-knack all over again. *(Clap your hands)*

(Chorus)

9. London Bridge *(Traditional Tune)*

London Bridge is falling down.
Falling down, falling down.
London Bridge is falling down.
My fair lady!

Build it up with iron bars,
Iron bars, iron bars.
Build it up with iron bars,
My fair lady!

Iron bars will bend and break.
Bend and break, bend and break.
Iron bars will bend and break.
My fair lady!

Here's a prisoner I have got.
I have got, I have got.
Here's a prisoner I have got.
My fair lady!

(Two children represent a bridge by facing each other, clasping hands, and holding them high for the others to pass under. The other players, holding each other by the hand, pass under the arch while the verses are sung by everyone playing. As the words are sung, the players representing the bridge drop their arms around the one who happens to be passing under at the time, and sing the verse swaying side to side. Start game over with two new different children representing the bridge.)

10. The Farmer In The Dell *(Traditional Tune)*

The farmer in the dell.
The farmer in the dell.
Heigh-o! the dairy-o!
The farmer in the dell.

The farmer takes a wife.
The farmer takes a wife.
Heigh-o! the dairy-o!
The farmer takes a wife.

The wife takes a child.
The wife takes a child.
Heigh-o! the dairy-o!
The wife takes a child.

Succeeding verses:
The child takes a nurse, etc.
The nurse takes a cat, etc.
The cat takes a rat, etc.
The rat takes the cheese, etc.

The players stand in circle with one of their number in the center who represents the farmer in the dell. At the singing of the second verse, where the farmer takes a wife, the center player beckons to another, who goes in and stands by her. The circle keeps moving while each verse is sung. Each time, the player last called in beckons to another; that is the wife beckons into the circle a child, the child beckons one for a nurse, etc., until six are standing in the circle. But when the lines 'the rat takes the cheese" are sung, the players inside the circle and those forming it jump up and down and clap their hands in a grand confusion, and the game breaks up.

11. Let's Play Automobile

Teacher reads the verses while the children act them out.

Time to take a little ride.
Open the door and get inside.
   (Everyone pretends to open door and sit down)
Now the engine starts to hum.
Shakes a bit, goes brr...brr...brrum!
   (Everyone on hands and knees, hums, shakes)
Then the tires go around.
Rolling faster on the ground.
(Everyone makes circles in the air with his arms)
Turn the steering wheel just so.
To take us where we want to go.
(Everyone turns a steering wheel)
Oooh! It's raining, splattering down!
Hear the windshield wiper's sound.
(Everyone nods head from side to side clucking tongues in rhythm)

Turn the lights on, see them blink!
Did you know headlights could wink?
   (Everyone winks)
My! This road is full of bumps.
Ups and down and, oops, more jumps!
   (Everyone jumps up and down)
Our gas tank's low, our tires need air.
Look! A station over there!
(Everyone point)
Listen to the air pump ring.
Psht, psht, air goes in, then ping!
   (Everyone imitates sounds)
From pump to hose to empty tank.
What a lot of gas we drank!
   (Everyone gurgles)
Time to turn around, and then,
Soon we'll all be home again.

12. Counting Rhyme

One, two, tie my shoe.
That is what I've learned to do.
Three, four, sit on the floor.
Hang my head. Pretend to snore.
Five, six, stir and mix.
With spoons, or maybe forks or sticks.
Seven, eight, set my bait.
Hang my pole, then sit and wait.
Nine, ten, that's the end.
It's so much fun when I pretend.

13. Listen And Do

Listen, listen.
We'll play a game.
When I snap my fingers,
Call out your name. *(Pause, then snap fingers)*

Listen, listen.
Put your hands on you head. *(Whisper)*
Now with one hand
Point to something...red.

Listen, listen.
Put one hand on your shoe. *(Whisper)*
Now with your other hand
Point to something...blue.

Listen, listen.
Put you hands behind your back. *(Whisper)*
Now with both your hands
Point to something...black.

Listen, listen.
What will we hear? *(Whisper)*
It's a lot of friendly noises.
As we give ourselves a cheer.
(Everyone claps and cheers)

14. Body Plays

a. Hopping

My shoes must go.
They're way too small
For a child like me,
A child so tall.
They pinch me so.
I hop and hop.
All over the place.
I just can't stop.

b. Marching

All the soldiers
March right past.
All in step.
From first to last.
Heads held high.
Chins tucked under.
Their marching boots
Sound like thunder.

c. Skipping

Hi, my brother,
And how are you?
Shake hands, my brother.
And tell me what's new.
Let's walk, my brother.
And then join hands.
To skip, my brother,
All over the land.

15. Chester, Have You Heard About Harry?

Chester, have you heard about Harry?
(Touch chest, ear and hair)
Just got back from the Ar-my.
*(Touch chest, back; right hand on left upper arm,
left thumb pointing to chest)*
I hear he knows how to wear a rose.
*(Point to eye, touch ear, touch nose,
frame hands above chest as if wearing a corsage)*
Hip, hip, hoo-ray.
*(Touch right hand to right hip, left hand to left hip
wave pointer fingers in the air)*
For the Ar-my.
*(Right hand on left upper arm
left thumb pointing to chest)*

16. Deep And Wide

Deep and wide. Deep and wide.
There's a fountain flowing deep and wide.
Deep and wide, deep and wide.
There's a fountain flowing deep and wide.

Motions: Use hands in front to describe words:
"Deep"—one hand above the other
"Wide—two palms facing each other
"Fountain"—both hands move upward
"Flowing"—hands move in ripple, waving motion.

17. Do Your Ears Hang Low?

Do your ears hang low? *(Thumb in each ear)*
Do they wobble to and fro? *(Shake palms together)*
Can you tie them in a knot? *(Tie knot)*
Can you tie them in a bow? *(Tie bow at neck)*
Can you throw them over your shoulder?
Like a continental soldier? *(Salute)*
Do your ears hang low?

Repeat three times, each time faster.

18. The Grand Old Duke of York

The grand old Duke of York.
He had ten thousand men.
He marched them up the hill, and *(Stand up)*
He marched them down again. *(Sit down)*
And when they're up, they're up *(Up)*
And when they're down, they're down *(Down)*
And when they're only halfway up *(Halfway, knees bent)*
They're neither up nor down.

19. This Is What I Can Do

This is what I can do.
This is what I can do.
This is what I can do.
Now I pass it on to you.
   (Each child leads a movement such as tapping foot, clapping, etc.)

20. Jack In The Box

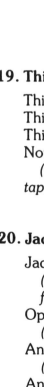

Jack in the box, Jack in the box.
   (Get into crouched position with hands folded over head like a lid)
Open the lid.
   (Lift arms off head. Pause)
And out he pops.
   (Jump up)
And we bounce and we bounce and we bounce and we bounce and we bounce together.

21. Jack Is Hiding

Jack is hiding down in his box.
   (Crouch down with arms over head like lid)
'Til someone opens the lid...pop!

22. Teddy Bear

Teddy Bear, Teddy Bear, turn around. *(Act out)*
Teddy Bear, Teddy Bear, touch the ground.
Teddy Bear, Teddy Bear, show one shoe.
Teddy Bear, Teddy Bear, you'd better skidoo. *(Walk quickly around)*

23. When I'm Up

When I'm up, I'm up.
And when I'm down, I'm down.
But when I'm only halfway up,
I'm neither up nor down.

24. Tippy Tippy Tiptoe

Tippy tippy tiptoe, off we go.
Tippy tippy tiptoe, to and fro.
Tippy tippy tiptoe, through the house.
Tippy tippy tiptoe, quiet as a mouse.

25. Body of Lesson   *(Do In Sing-Song Fashion)*

See-saw, up and down,
In the air and on the ground.
Swing, swing, swing so high.
I can nearly touch the sky.
Rain, rain go away.
Come again another day.
Bye, bye, baby-o.
Now it's time to sleep you go.
Star light, star bright,
First star I see tonight.
I wish I may.
I wish I might.
Make this wish come true tonight.

26. Strawberry Shortcake

Strawberry shortcake. Huckleberry Finn.
When you hear your birth month. you jump in.
January. February. March. etc.
When you hear your birth month. you jump out.
January. February. March. etc.

27. Sandy Maloney

Here we go Sandy Maloney. Here we go Sandy Maloney.
Here we go Sandy Maloney, and turn yourself around.
Clap your hands on your knees now. Clap your hands on your hands now.
Clap your hands on your knees now, and turn yourself around.

Teacher and/or children make up other verses. For example: tap hands on head, jump up high in the air, etc.

28. Popcorn Pop *(Chanting Rhythm)*

This should be acted out by the children.
Popcorn popping means you can jump around.

Pop, pop, popcorn, pop.
Give a little pop 'till you hit the top.
Popcorn good for my tummy.
Now you roll around in butter
'Til you're warm and yummy.

Pop, pop, popcorn, pop.
I think you must be ready.
'Cause I see you've stopped.
Pour on the salt.
About a quarter of a cup.
Then I'll get you in my fingers.
And I'll eat you all up.

29. Grandma's Glasses

Here are Grandma's glasses. *(Fingers around eyes)*
Here is Grandma's hat. *(Hands on head)*.
This is the way she folds her hands. *(Folds hands)*
And lays them in her lap. *(Fold hands in lap)*
Here are Grandpa's glasses. *(Larger glasses)*
Here is Grandpa's hat. *(Larger hat)*
This is the way he folds his arms. *(Across chest)*
Just like that. *(With emphasis)*

30. Knock, Knock

Knock, knock. *(Knock on child's forehead)*
Peek in. *(Open eyes wider)*
Open the latch. *(Push up tip of nose)*
And walk right in. *(Walk fingers into mouth)*
How do you do Mr. Chin, Chin, Chin? *(Wiggle chin)*

31. Stretching

I am stretching very tall. *(Stretch up)*
And now I'm shrinking very small. *(Squat position)*
Now tall, now small.
Now I'm a tiny ball. *(Ball up)*

32. Peter Hammers

Peter hammers with one hammer,
 one hammer, one hammer.
 (Pound one fist on the floor)
Peter hammers with one hammer.
All day long.

Peter hammers with two hammers.
 (Two fists)
Peter hammers with three hammers.
 (Two fists, one foot)
Peter hammers with four hammers.
 (Two fists, two feet)
Peter hammers with five hammers.
 (Two fists, two feet, head).
Peter's very tired now......
 (Rub eyes, then lay head on hands.)

33. If You're Happy

If you're happy and you know it, clap your hands. *(clap, clap)*
If you're happy and you know it, clap your hands. *(clap, clap)*
If you're happy and you know it,
Then your face will surely show it.
If you're happy and you know it, clap your hands. *(Clap, clap)*

Extras: tap feet, nod head, wiggle fingers, turn around, etc.

34. Ten In The Bed *(Use Ten Fingers)*

There were ten in the bed and the little one said, "roll over, roll over".
So they all rolled over and one fell off. *(Roll arms around each other)*
There were nine in the bed and the little one said, "roll over, roll over".
So they all rolled over and one fell off.
There were eight in the bed and the little one said, "roll over, roll over".
So they all rolled over and one fell off.
There were seven in the bed and the little one said, "roll, over, roll over".
So they all rolled over and one fell off.
There were six in the bed and the little one said, "roll over, roll over".
So they all rolled over and one fell off.
There were five in the bed and the little one said, "roll over, roll over"
So they all rolled over and one fell off.
There were four in the bed and the little one said, "roll over, roll over".
So they all rolled over and one fell off.
There were three in the bed and the little one said, "roll over, roll over".
So they all rolled over and one fell off.
There were two in the bed and the little one said, "roll over, roll over".
So they all rolled over and one fell off, and the last one said
    "Oh, boy, now I can stretch".

35. Pop! Pop! Pop!

Pop! Pop! Pop! *(Clap hands)*
Pour the corn into the pot.
Pop! Pop! Pop! *(Clap hands)*
Take and shake it 'til it's hot.
Pop! Pop! Pop! *(Clap hands)*
Lift the lid—what have we got?
Pop! Pop! Pop! *(Clap hands)*
Popcorn! *(Say loudly)*

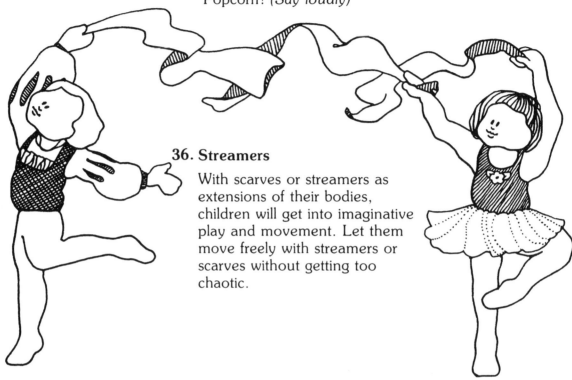

36. Streamers

With scarves or streamers as extensions of their bodies, children will get into imaginative play and movement. Let them move freely with streamers or scarves without getting too chaotic.

37. Simon Says

The teacher gives directions to children such as jump up and down, turn around, hop, etc., but the children can only do these movements if Simon says to do them. If a child **does** it without Simon saying to, he is out and must sit down.

38. Memory Games

The teacher introduces a sound with a corresponding movement. For example: a tambourine is the signal for the children to move their hips in a circular movement. After giving several clues, combine the sounds so the children can act it out.

39. Duck, Duck, Goose

Children sit in a big circle. One child is chosen to be the goose. The goose walks around the circle clockwise, tapping each child on the head saying "duck, duck, duck", and finally saying "goose".

The new goose gets up and chases the old goose around the circle as the old goose tries to get back to his seat before being caught.

40. Freeze Game

The tambourine or drum indicates when the children are to move around freely. Then the teacher stops playing and says "freeze". The children stop motionless in their tracks.

41. Opposite Game *(For Older Children)*

The teacher will give commands and the children will do the opposite. For example: "sit down" and the children will stand up.

42. Pretzel

Stand in a circle, holding hands. Without letting go of you hands, see how twisted up you can get—like a pretzel!

43. Stand up, Sit Down

Sit on the ground, holding on, like this:

Now try to stand up without letting go.

Now can you sit down again?

44. Turtle Tag

Turtle tag is played just like regular tag, but on the stomach. Start in a triangle. The person in the middle is "it". Someone says "go!". The "it" turtle tries to catch the other turtles. Children must stay on their stomachs.

45. Follow The Pattern

The teacher selects a specific movement pattern and rhythm. An example of such a movement pattern would be:

1. slap thighs twice

2. touch shoulders twice

3. pat head twice, repeat

The variations to this activity are endless.

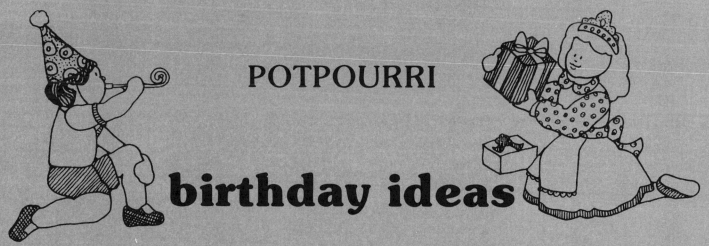

POTPOURRI

birthday ideas

Here are some unique birthday ideas to try. Have a Happy Birthday!

1. **a.** Children are sitting in a circle and we point out birthday child. Ask the child what kind of cake she wants. Teacher says "Today is _____ birthday. Let's make her a cake."Take hand and mix and stir as you say "mix and stir, stir and mix and into the oven to bake. Here is our cake so nice and round." *(Motion circle with arms).* "Let's frost it, *(pretend to frost it)* with chocolate and white" *(or whatever the child has chosen).* "We put five candles on it to make a birthday light" *(place candles).*

   b. Children are sitting in a circle and the birthday person is pointed out. Teacher says "Let's pretend to open some gifts". *(Make motions of untying the bow or unwrapping the paper, etc.)* Each child then must act out what his present is. For example: a Jack-in-the—box, a ball, etc. Others must try to guess what it is.

   c. Birthday child stands up and tapes his name on a birthday calendar and then faces the other children. The teacher asks the child to hold up as many fingers as his age is while everyone counts the fingers or years together. The group then sings "Happy Birthday" to the child.

   d. Make a giant birthday cake out of construction paper and put it on a wall or bulletin board. Each time a child has a birthday, he can put a candle with his name on it on the cake. Candles can be made by the children or cut out ahead of time by the teachers. Everyone sings "Happy Birthday" to the child.

2. **My Birthday Cake**

   My birthday cake is pink and white.
   (Make a circle with arms).
   The lighted candles make it bright.
   One, two, three, four, five pink candles.
   (Hold up fingers one by one to represent candles)
   What a pretty sight.

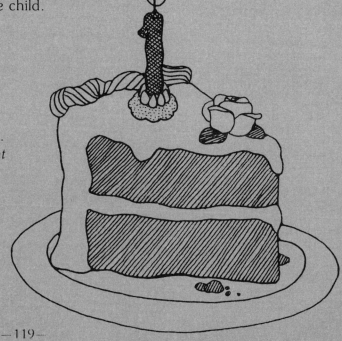

3. Polly's Birthday

Polly had a birthday.
Polly had a cake. *(Make a circle with arms)*
Polly's mother made it. *(Action of stirring)*
Polly watched it bake.
Frosting on the top. *(Right hand held out, palm down)*
Frosting in between. *(Left hand moves under right palm)*
Oh, it was the nicest cake
That you have ever seen!
Polly had some candles.
One, two, three, four, five. *(Hold up fingers one at a time)*
Who can tell how many years
Polly's been alive?

4. Birthday Candles

Solo: Today I have a birthday.
I'm six years old you see.
And here I have a birthday cake.
    (Make a circle with thumbs and forefingers)
Which you may share with me.
First we count the candles.
All: One, two, three, four, five, six.
    (Hold up fingers one by one)
The counting now is done.
Solo: Let's snuff out the candles.
Out each flame will go.
All: WH...Wh...Wh...Wh...Wh...Wh...
And one by one we blow.

5. Five Little Candles

Five little candles on a birthday cake.
    (Hold up five fingers)
Just five, and not one more.
You may blow one candle out.
Wh! And that leaves four.
    (Bend down one finger)
Four little candles on a birthday dake.
    (Hold up four fingers)
As gay as they could be.
You may blow one candle out.
Wh! And that leaves three.

Three little candles on a birthday cake.
Standing straight and true.
You may blow one candle out.
Wh! And that leaves two.
Two little candles on a birthday cake.
Helping us have fun.
You may blow the candles out.
Wh! And that leaves one.
One little candle on a birthday cake.
It knows its task is done.
You may blow the candle out.
Wh! And that leaves none.

the seasons

To help introduce each season, here are some clever ideas which will enhance your curriculum and describe each season.

1. Autumn

a. Ten Red Apples

Ten red apples grow on a tree.
(Both hands high)
Five for you and five for me.
(Dangle one hand and then the other)
Let us shake the tree just so.
(Shake body)
And ten red apples will fall below.
(Hands fall)
1,2,3,4,5,6,7,8,9,10.
(Count each finger)

b. Ten Rosy Apples

Ten rosy apples high in a tree.
(Arms above head, fingers separated)
Safely hiding where no one can see.
When the wind comes rocking to and fro.
(Arms sway above head)
Ten rosy apples to the ground must go.
(Apples tumble down to the floor).

c. In The Apple Tree

Away up high in an apple tree. *(Point up)*
Two red apples smiled at me. *(Form circles with fingers)*
I shook that tree as hard as I could. *(Shake tree)*
Down came the apples and m-m-m-they were good.
(Rub stomach)

d. When The Leaves Are On The Ground

When the leaves are on the ground.*(Point to floor)*
Instead of on the trees. *(Hands clasped over head)*
I like to make a great big pile of them.
Way up to my knees. *(Hands on knees)*
I like to run and jump in them. *(Jump once)*
And kick them all around. *(Kicking motion with foot)*
I like the prickly feel of them.
And the crickly, crackly sound. *(Click fingernails)*
The leaves are green, the nuts are brown. *(Raise arms sideward, wiggle fingers, make circles for nuts)*
They hang so high they will never fall down. *(Stretch arms)*
Leave them alone 'til the bright fall weather. *(Move hands as if wind blows softly)*
And then they will all come down together. *(Bring arms down to side quickly)*

e. Leaves Are Floating Down

Leaves are floating softly down.
   (Flutter fingers)
They make a carpet on the ground.
Then, swish! The wind comes whirling by.
   (Bring hand around rapidly)
And sends them dancing to the sky.
   (Flutter fingers upward)

f. Little Leaves

Little leaves fall gently down.
Red and yellow and orange and brown.
   (Flutter fingers)
Whirling, whirling 'round and 'round.
Quietly without a sound.
Falling softly to the ground.
   (Lower bodies gradually to floor)
Down, down, down, and down.

g. Five Red Apples

Five red apples in a grocery store. *(Hold up five fingers)*
Bobby bought one, and then there were four. *(Bend down one finger)*
Four red apples on an apple tree.
Susie ate one, and then there were three. *(Bend down one finger)*
Three red apples. What did Alice do?
Why, she ate one, and there were two. *(Bend down one finger)*
Two red apples ripening in the sun.
Timmy ate one, and then there was one. *(Bend down one finger)*
One red apple and now we are done.
I ate the last one, and now there are none. *(Bend down last finger)*

2. Winter

a. Mr. Snowman

Mr. Snowman so big and fat.
All dressed up in your Sunday hat.
A stick for a nose and coal for eyes.
My you look so proud and wise.
Mr. Snowman the sun is hot.
You will melt as likely as not.
When you are little, ya know what then?
We will build you up again.

b. I'm So Glad It's Snowing

I'm so glad it's snowing, tra la la la.
I'll shovel the snow in the front yard.
I'll shovel the snow in the back yard.
   (Make shoveling motions)
I'm so glad it's snowing, tra la la la la.

c. Little Pig

(With pointer finger of right hand, touch fingers and thumb of left hand, starting with little finger)

This little pig lost his sweater.
This little pig lost her muff.
Said this little pig, "Jack Frost will catch you."
Said this little pig, "Sure enough."
Said this little pig, "Br-r-r-r wee, wee, wee.
This nice warm house is the place for me.
   (Put thumb in fist)

d. Jack Frost

Jack Frost is a fairy small.
　(Show smallness with thumb and pointer)
I'm sure he is out today.
He nipped my nose.
　(Point to nose)
And pinched my toes.
　(Point to toes)
When I went out to play.

e. I Am A Snowman

Now I am a snowman.
　(Stand with arms out)
Standing on the lawn.
I melt and melt and melt.
And pretty soon I'm gone.
　(Body slumps and voice fades)

f. Gather Snow

Gather snow and make a ball. *(Hands in ball formation)*
Make a snowman round and tall. *(Indicate with hands)*
Coal for buttons. *(Pretend to place buttons)*
Coal for eyes. *(Pretend to place eyes)*
There he stands and looks so wise. *(Stand like a snowman)*

g. Chubby Little Snowman

A chubby little snowman.
Had a carrot nose.
　(Point to nose)
Along came a bunny.
And what do you suppose?
　*(Hold up two fingers on right
　hand to make bunny)*
That hungry little bunny
Looking for his lunch.
Ate that little snowman's nose.
　(Pretend to grab nose)
Nibble, nibble, crunch.

h. Snowman In Our Yard

We made a snowman in our yard.
Jolly and round and fat.
　(Hold hands under stomach and jiggle it)
We gave him Father's pipe to smoke.
　(Pretend to hold pipe)
And Father's battered hat.
　(Tap top of head)
We tied a scarf around his neck.
　(Pretend to tie scarf)
And in his buttonhole.

We stuck a holly sprag.
　(Pretend to put holly in buttonhole)
We had black buttons of coal.
　(Indicate buttons)
He had black eyes, a turned up nose.
　(Indicate eyes and nose)
A wide and cheerful grin.
And there he stood in our front yard.
　(Stand tall)
Inviting company in!
　(Make motion with hand)

i. One Little, Two Little, Three Little Snowmen

One little, two little, three little snowmen.
  (Hold up one finger for each snowman)
Four little, five little, six little snowmen.
Seven little, eight little, nine little snowmen.
Ten little snowmen bright.

Reverse.

j. I'm A Little Snowman *(Tune: "I'm A Little Teapot")*

I'm a little snowman, short and fat.
Here is my broomstick, here is my hat
When the sun comes out, I melt away.
Down, down, down, down, whoops....
I'm a puddle.

k. Snowman

Roll a snowball large.
  (Arms make circle)
Then one middle size.
  (Two pointer fingers and two thumbs make a circle)
Roll a snowball small.
  (One pointer and thumb)
Use lumps of coal for eyes.
  (Point to eyes)
An old hat upon his head.
  (Place both hands on top of head)
And for his necktie, tie around
  (Motion of tying ribbon)
A corn cob pipe goes in his mouth.
  (Point to mouth)
Some buttons on his vest.
  (Point to buttons down front)
Of snowmen, he's the best!

l. Little Snowman

I make a little snowman.
With hat and cane complete. *(Hold out hand to indicate little snowman)*
With shiny buttons on his coat.
And shoes upon his feet. *(Indicate buttons and shoes)*
But I know when the sun comes out
My snowman will go away. *(Make circle with arms)*
So I'll put him in our big deep freeze.
And he'll be sure to stay.

m. I Am A Snowman

I am a snowman, cold and white.
I stand so still through all the night. *(Stand still)*
With a carrot nose. *(Point to nose)*
And head held high
And a lump of coal to make each eye. *(Point to eye)*
I have a muffler made of red.
And a stovepipe hat upon my head. *(Place hands on top of head)*
The sun is coming out! Oh my!
I think that I am going to cry. *(Start sinking to the floor)*
Yesterday, I was so plump and round.
Now I'm just a river on the ground. *(Sink to the floor)*

3. Spring

a. Rain, Rain, Go Away *(Traditional Tune)*

Rain, rain, go away.
Come again another day.
Little Suzie wants to play.
Rain, rain, go away.

b. There is Thunder *(Tune: "Are You Sleeping")*

There is thunder. There is thunder.
Hear it roar. Hear it roar.
Pitter, patter, rain drops.
Pitter, patter, rain drops.
I'm all wet! I'm all wet!

c. It's Raining *(Tune: "Rain, Rain, Go Away")*

It's raining, it's pouring,
The old man is snoring.
He went to bed and bumped his head.
And couldn't get up in the morning.

d. Five Little Robins

Five little robins up in a tree.
Father, mother *(Thumb, pointer)*
And babies three. *(Middle, ring and little fingers)*
Father caught a bug. *(Point to thumb)*
Mother caught a worm. *(Point to pointer)*
This one got the bug. *(Middle finger)*
This one got the worm. *(Ring finger)*
This one said, "Now it's my turn". *(Little finger)*

e. The Seed Story

(This should be acted out)

You are a seed buried in the ground.
You feel wet and warm under the ground.
The sun is shining very bright.
You slowly begin to crack open the seed.
You are beginning to grow.
You are slowly growing up through the ground.
Your leaves start to open.
You are growing bigger, wider, and taller.
The sun is covered by a huge rain cloud.
You are cold.
The wind begins to blow.

The rain begins to fall.
You are blown from side to side.
The rain is pounding you down to the ground.
The ground is muddy and wet.
You feel heavy and wet and tired.
Suddenly the rain stops and the wind stops.
The sun is bright again.
You slowly lift yourself from the ground.
You open your leaves to dry them in the sun.
You are warm again from the sun.

f. How Does Your Garden Grow?

Corn stalks grow high, way up in the sky.
    (Raise arms above head and sway back and forth)
Watermelons are round,
    (Arms in front with fingers interlocking)
And grow on the ground.
    (Point to floor)
But under the ground,
    (Tap floor with finger)
Where no one can see.
Grow potatoes and onions and carrots.
    (Raise three fingers consecutively)
All three.
    (Show three fingers you raised)

I plant a little seed.
    (Place left finger in the palm of right hand.)
In the dark, dark ground.
Out comes the yellow sun, big and round.
    (Raise arms above head and fingers interlock)
Down comes the cool rain, soft and slow.
    (Wiggle fingers down in front of you.)
Up comes the little seed—grow, grow, GROW.
    (Push pointer finger of left hand through fist of right hand)

g. Ten Little Pigeons

Ten little pigeons sat in a line.
  (Hands stretched up over head)
Up on the barn in the warm sunshine.
Ten little pigeons flew down to the ground.
  (Flutters fingers down)
And ate the crumbs that were lying on the ground.

h. Five Little Sparrows

Five Little sparrows high in a tree.. *(Hold one hand up)*
The first one said "Whom do I see?" *(Point to thumb)*
The second one said "I see the street." *(Pointed finger)*
The third one said "And seed to eat". *(Middle finger)*
The fourth one said "The seeds are wheat". *(Ring finger)*
The fifth one said "Tweet, tweet, tweet". *(Little finger)*

i. Five Little May Baskets

Five little May baskets waiting by the door. *(Hold up five fingers)*
One will go to Mrs. Smith and then there will be four. *(Bend down one finger)*
Four little May baskets, pretty as can be.
One will go to Mrs. Brown and then there will be three. *(Bend down one finger)*
It will go to Mr. Jones, then there will be two. *(Bend down one finger)*
Two little May baskets yellow as the sun.
One will go to Mr. Black, then there will be one. *(Bend down one finger)*
One little May basket. It's sure to go
To my own Mother, who's the nicest one I know. *(Cup hands to form basket)*

j. Pitter, Patter

Oh, where do you come from
You little drops of rain.
Pitter, patter, pitter, patter
  (Tap fingers on table or floor)
Down the window pane.
Tell me, little raindrops,
Is that the way you play?
Pitter, patter, pitter, patter
  (Tap fingers as before)
All the rainy day.

k. Rain

The storm came up so very quick.
It couldn't have been quicker.
I should have brought my hat along.
  (Place flat palm on top of head)
I should have brought my slicker.
  (Indicate slicker)
My hair is wet, my feet are wet.
(Point to head and feet)
I couldn't be much wetter.
I fell into a river once.
But this is even wetter.

l. Rose

I like to pretend that I am a rose. *(Cup hands)*
That grows and grows and grows and grows. *(Open hands slowly)*
My hands are a rosebud closed up tight. *(Close hands)*
With not a tiny speck of light.
Then slowly the petals open for me. *(Let hands come apart gradually)*
And here is a full-grown rose, you see!

m. Popcorn Popping On the Apricot Tree

(This can be chanted)

I look out the window
And what do I see.
Popcorn popping on the apricot tree.
Spring has brought me such a nice surprise.
Popcorn blossoms popping right before my eyes.

I can take a handful and make a treat.
Popcorn balls that would smell so sweet.
It really isn't so,
But it seems to me,
There's popcorn popping on the apricot tree.

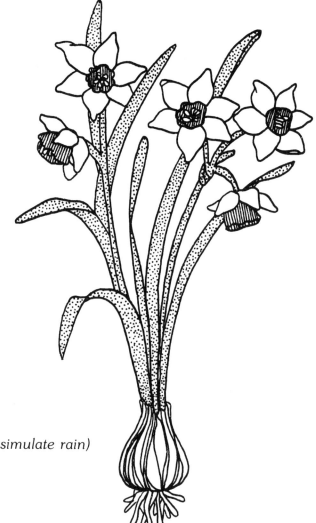

n. Five Little Flowers

Five little flowers
Stand in the sun.
  (Hold up five fingers)
See their heads nodding.
Bowing, one by one.
  (Bend fingers)
Down, down, down.
Comes the gentle rain.
  (Raise hands, wiggle fingers, and lower arms to simulate rain)
And the five little flowers
Lift their heads again!
  (Hold up five fingers)

o. Purple Violets

One purple violet in our garden grew. *(Hold up one finger)*
Up popped another, and that made two. *(Hold up two fingers)*
Two purple violets were all that I could see.
But Billy found another, and that made three. *(Hold up three fingers)*
Three purple violets,—if I could find one more,
I'd make a wreath for Mother and that would make four. *(Hold up four fingers)*
Four purple violets, sure as you're alive!
Why, here is another! And now there are five!
(Hold up five fingers)

p. The Wind

The wind came out to play one day.
He swept the clouds out of his way. *(Sweeping motion with arms)*
He blew the leaves and away they flew. *(Fluttering motion)*
The trees bend low and their branches did, too. *(Lift arms and lower them)*
The wind blew the great big ships at sea. *(Repeat sweeping motion)*
The wind blew my kite away from me.

q. Raindrops

Raindrops, raindrops.
Falling all around.
Pitter, patter on the rooftops
Pitter, patter on the ground.
Here is an umbrella.
It will keep me dry.
When I go walking in the rain.
I hold it up so high.

Pitter, patter, raindrops.
Falling from the sky.
Here is my umbrella.
To keep me safe and dry!
When the rain is over,
And the sun begins to glow.
Little flowers start to bud.
And grow and grow and grow!

4. Summer

a. You Are My Sunshine *(Traditional Tune)*

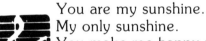

You are my sunshine.
My only sunshine.
You make me happy when skies are gray.
You'll never know, dear,
How much I love you.
Please don't take my sunshine away.

b. Little Brown Seed

I'm a little brown seed in the ground.
Rolled up in a tiny ball.
   (Sitting on heels, on the floor, drop head over knees)
I'll wait for the rain and sunshine.
   (In the same position, place arms over head and wiggle fingers downward for rain.
Then place both hands in large circle over head for sun)
To make me big and tall.
   (Stand straight, stretching arms over head).

c. My Garden

This is my garden. *(Extend one hand forward, palm up)*
I'll rake it with care. *(Make raking motion on palm with three fingers of other hand)*
And then some flower seeds *(Planting motion)*
I'll plant in there.
The sun will shine. *(Make circle with hands)*
And the rain will fall. *(Let fingers flutter down to lap)*
And my garden will blossom. *(Cup hands together, extend upward slowly)*
And grow straight and tall.

d. The Little Plant

In the heart of a seed,
Buried deep, so deep.
A dear little plant.
Lay fast asleep.

Wake! said the sunshine.
And creep to the light.
Wake! said the voice
Of the raindrops bright.

The little plant heard.
And rose to see.
What the wonderful
Outside world might be.

leftovers

Leftovers are always good and below are some we could never do without. Your kids will love them too.

1. On Top Of Spaghetti *(Tune: "On Top Of Old Smokey")*

On top of spaghetti, all covered with cheese.
I lost my poor meatball, when somebody sneezed.
It rolled off the table, and onto the floor.
And then my poor meatball rolled right out of the door.
It rolled in the garden, and under a bush.
And then my poor meatball was nothing but mush.
That mush was so tasty, as tasty could be.
Early that summer, it grew into a tree.
The tree was all covered with such lovely moss.
It grew lots of meatballs and tomato sauce.
So if you eat spaghetti all covered with cheese,
Hold on to your meatball, and don't ever sneeze.

2. John Jacob Jingleheimer Smith *(Traditional Tune)*

John Jacob Jingleheimer Smith. His name is my name too.
Whenever he goes out, the people always shout.
John Jacob Jingleheimer Smith. DA DA DA DA DA DA DA.

Repeat four times getting quieter each time until the last time is silent. "DA DA DA" at the end is very loud each time.

3. Popeye The Sailor Man *(Traditional Tune)*

I'm Popeye the Sailor Man.
I live in a garbage can.
I'm strong to the finish
'Cause I eat my spinach.
I'm Popeye the Sailor Man.

4. The Little Skunk *(Chant)*

Oh, I stuck my head in a little skunk's hole.
And the little skunk said, "Gosh darn your soul".
Take it out. *(Clap, clap)*
Take it out. *(Clap, clap)*
Re—move it!
Well, I didn't take it out.
And the little skunk said,
"If you don't take it out, you'd wish you had".
Take it out. *(Clap, clap)*
Take it out. *(Clap, clap)*
Psss—sssssss————sssssssst.
I removed it too late. *(Sing this line pinching nose with fingers)*

5. Take Me Out To The Ball Game *(Traditional Tune)*

Take me out to the ball game.
Take me out to the fair.
Buy me some peanuts and crackerjack.
I don't care if I never get back.
We will root, root root for the home team.
If they don't win, it's a shame.
For it's one-two-three strikes, you're out.
At the old ball game.

6. The Cuckoo Song *(Traditional Tune)*

Oh, I went to Peter's flowing spring.
Where the water's so good.
And I heard there the cuckoo.
As she called from the wood.

(Chorus)
Ho-le-rah, ho-le-rah-ki-ki-rah,
Ho-le-rah ku-kuck
Ho-le-rah-ki-ki-ah, ho-le-rah-ku-kuck;
Ho-le-rah-ki-ki-ah, ho-le-rah-ku-kuck;
Ho-le-rah-ki-ki-ah, ho

After Easter come sunny days.
That will melt all the snow.
Then I'll marry my maiden fair.
Who'll be happy, I know!

(Chorus)

When I've married my maiden fair,
What than can I desire?
Oh, a home for her tending
And some wood for the fire.

(Chorus)

(Motions: Drum knees on each syllable of "Ho-le-rah". Then slap knee on "ho", clap hands on "le-rah", and snap fingers on "ki-ki-rah". Slap knee on "Ho", clap hands on "le-rah", and snap fingers on ku-kuck".)

7. The Happy Wanderer *(Traditional Tune)*

I love to go a-wandering along the mountain track.
And as I go, I love to sing, my knapsack on my back.

(Chorus)
Val de ri, val de ra, val de ra
Val de ra ha ha ha ha ha
Val de ri, val di ra. **My knapsack on my back.**

I wave my hand to all I meet, and they wave back to me.
And blackbirds call so loud and sweet, from every greenwood tree.

(Repeat chorus)

Oh, may I go a-wandering until the day I die.
Oh, may I always laugh and sing, beneath God's clean blue sky.

(Repeat chorus)

8. The Opposite Song

(Guitar chords: D and A; autoharp chords: G and D7)

I can say up,
And I can say down.
I can say smile,
And I can say frown.

I can say large.
And I can say small.
I can say short.
And I can say tall.

I can say black,
And I can say white.
I can say day,
And I can say night.

I can say yes.
And I can say no.
I can say fast.
And I can say slow.

I can say happy
And I can say sad.
I can say good.
And I can say bad.

I can say wet.
And I can say dry.
I can say laugh.
And I can say cry.

Well, I can say young.
And I can say old.
I can say hot.
And I can say cold.

I can say south.
And I can say north.
I can say back.
And I can say forth.

I can say bottom.
And I can say top.
I can say start.
And I can say STOP!

9. Hokey Pokey *(Traditional Tune)*

(This should be acted out by the children by following the directive words.)

You put your right arm in.
You put your right arm out.
You put your right arm in.
And you shake it all about.
You do the Hokey Pokey *(Wave arms overhead and shuffle feet)*
And you turn yourself around.
That's what it's all about. *(Clapping)*

Continue with left arm, right foot, left foot, right hip, left hip, bottom, head, whole self.

Last verse:
You do the Hokey Pokey
You do the Hokey Pokey.
You do the Hokey Pokey,
That's what it's all about.

10. Aiken-Drum

A teacher can draw the Aiken-Drum person while the song is being sung.

There was a man who lived in the moon.
Lived in the moon,
Lived in the moon.
There was a man who lived in the moon.
And they called him Aiken-Drum.

His face was an apple, *(Children name a food)*
An apple,
An apple,
His face was an apple.
And they called him Aiken-Drum.

(Chorus)
And he played upon a ladle,
A ladle,
A ladle,
He played upon a ladle.
And they called him Aiken-Drum.

His eyes were two raisins,
Two raisins,
Two raisins
His eyes were two raisins,
And they called him Aiken-Drum.

(Chorus)

Wasn't he a yummy man,
A yummy man.
A yummy man.
Wasn't he a yummy man,
And they called him Aiken-Drum.

(Chorus)

Move on to nose, mouth, hair, tummy, arms, legs, etc.

11. Beans In Your Ears

My mother said not to put beans in my ears, beans in my ears, beans in my ears,
My mother said not to put beans in my ears, beans in my ears.
Now why should I want to put beans in my ears?
Hey! Maybe its fun to put beans in our ears.
Sorry, I can't hear. I've got beans in my ears.

12. A Sailor

A sailor went to sea, sea, sea. *(Clap on all seas)*
To see what he could see, see, see. *(Clap on all sees)*
But all that he could see, see, see
Was the bottom of the deep blue sea, sea, sea.

(Replace claps with head nods, knee pats, stomps, etc.)

13. Long-Legged Sailor *(Chant)*

Did you ever, ever, ever in your long-legged life
See a long-legged sailor with a long-legged wife?
No *(or yes)* I never, never, never in my long-legged life
Saw a long-legged sailor with a long-legged wife.

Other verses: short-legged, bow-legged, two-legged, etc.

14. Miss Mary Mack

Miss Mary Mack, Mack, Mack *(Clap, clap, clap)*
All dressed in black, black, black *(Clap, clap, clap)*
With silver buttons, buttons, buttons *(Clap, clap, clap)*
Up and down her back, back, back.
She asked her mother, mother, mother
For fifty cents, cents, cents,
To see the elephant, elephant, elephant
Jump over the fence, fence, fence.
He jumped so high, high, high.
He touched the sky, sky, sky.
And didn't come back, back, back.
'Til the Fourth of July, 'ly, 'ly.
He jumped so low, low, low.
He stubbed his toe, toe, toe.
And that was the end, end, end,
Of the elephant show, show, show.

15. Four-Leaf Clover *(Traditional Tune)*

I'm looking over a four-leaf clover.
That I overlooked before.
One leaf is sunshine. The second is rain.
Third is the roses that grow in the lane.
Oh, there's no need explaining the one remaining
Is someone that I adore. I'm looking over
A four-leaf clover that I overlooked before.

16. Hello Hello

Teacher asks question and children answer "Sir".

T: Hello, hello, hello.
C: Sir.
T: Would you come out to play?
C: Sir.
T: No.
C: Sir.
T: Why?
C: Sir.
T: Because I've got a cold.
C: Sir.
T: Where'd you get your cold?
C: Sir.
T: At the North Pole.
C: Sir.

T: What were you doing there?
C: Sir.
T: Catching polar bears.
C: Sir.
T: How many did you catch?
C: Sir.
T: One.
C: Sir.
T: Two.
C: Sir.
T: Three.
C: Sir.
T: And that's enough for me.
C: Sir.

17. One, Two

One, two buckle my shoe.
Three, four shut the door.
Five, six pick up sticks.
Seven, eight lay them straight.
Nine, ten a big fat hen.

18. Choc'late Ice Cream

Choc'late ice cream. Ham on rye.
hot dog, french fries, raspberry pie.

19. Peas Porridge Hot

Peas porridge hot.
Peas porridge cold.
Peas porridge in the pot.
Nine days old.
Some like it hot.
Some like it cold.
Some like it in the pot
Nine days old.

20. Raggedy Doll

The raggedy doll said, "I don't mind
If my pants are held with a pin behind.
Or that the sawdust is out of my toe,
'Cause I'm just a raggedy doll, you know.

My arms are so floppy, they fling and flap.
And my head rests all the way down in my lap.

The rest of me goes to and fro.
'Cause I'm just a raggedy doll you know.

If somebody pulled me up by a string,
I'd stand so straight I'd certainly sing.
But my legs are so wobbly they just let go.
'Cause I'm just a raggedy doll, you know.

I can't move a muscle. I can just smile.
I just have to stay here for a long, long while.

I feel so soft from my head to my toe.
'Cause I'm just a raggedy doll, you know."

21. Jack-In-The-Box

(Use as a finger play by doubling up fist and releasing on the word "jump".)

Jack-in-the-box all shut up tight.
Not a breath of air. Not a peep of light.
How tired he must be, all in a hump.
Open the lid and out he'll jump.

22. Geiger Counter

Have children sit in a circle Lotus style. Use a bean bag or another small object to be designated as a valuable "gem" or piece of "gold". The "gold" is to be hidden in the lap of one of the children in the circle.

Another child is chosen to be "it" and leaves the room while the "gold" is hidden. When "it" returns, he is to find the "gold" by listening to the "geiger counter". The "geiger counter" is the circle of children themselves who clap slowly and softly when "it" is far away from the "gold". As "it" gets closer to the "gold" the children clap louder and faster until "it" is directly over the person whose lap the "gold" is hidden in. That person now becomes "it" and the game continues.

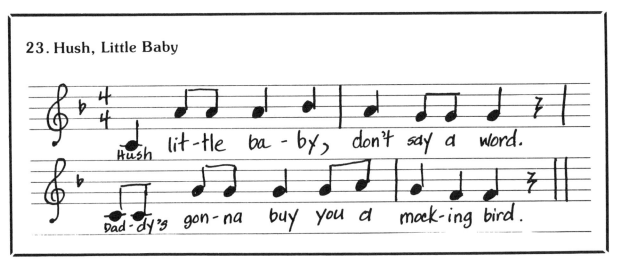

23. Hush, Little Baby

Hush lit-tle ba-by, don't say a word.
Dad-dy's gon-na buy you a mock-ing bird.

2. If that mocking bird don't sing,
   Daddy's gonna buy you a diamond ring.
3. If that diamond ring turns to brass.
   Daddy's gonna buy you a looking glass.
4. If that looking glass gets broke.
   Daddy's gonna buy you a billy goat.
5. If that billy goat don't pull,
   Daddy's gonna buy you a cart and bull.
6. If that cart and bull turn over
   Daddy's gonna buy you a dog named Rover.
7. If that dog named Rover don't bark,
   Daddy's gonna buy you a horse and cart.
8. If that horse and cart break down,
   You still will be the sweetest little baby in town.

24. Boom! Boom!

INDEX OF TITLES AND SUBJECTS

INDEX OF FIRST LINES FOR CHANTS, FINGERPLAYS, POEMS, SONGS